DATE DUE

GAYLORD		PRINTED IN U.S.A.

by the same author

Looking on Darkness
An Instant in the Wind
Rumours of Rain
A Dry White Season
A Chain of Voices
The Wall of the Plague

Writing in a State of Siege

Essays on Politics and Literature

ANDRÉ BRINK

SUMMIT BOOKS

NEW YORK

Copyright © 1983 by André Brink

Published by SUMMIT BOOKS
A Division of Simon & Schuster, Inc.
Simon & Schuster Building
1230 Avenue of the Americas
New York, New York 10020

First published in Great Britain in 1983 as
Mapmakers: Writing in a State of Siege by Faber and Faber Limited

SUMMIT BOOKS and colophon are trademarks of Simon & Schuster, Inc.

Manufactured in the United States of America

1 3 5 7 9 10 8 6 4 2
1 3 5 7 9 10 8 6 4 2 Pbk.

Library of Congress Cataloging in Publication Data

Brink, André Philippus, date.
Writing in a state of siege.

Collection, of articles, lectures, and speeches.
Bibliography: p.
1. Brink, André Philippus, 1935-   —Political
and social views—Addresses, essays, lectures.
2. South Africa—Politics and government—1961-   —Ad-
dresses, essays, lectures. 3. Politics and literature—
South Africa—Addresses, essays, lectures. I. Title.
PT6592.12.R5A6   1986   839.3'635   85-30265
ISBN 0-671-47751-X
ISBN 0-671-62289-7 Pbk.

. . . the struggle of man against power is the struggle of memory against forgetting.

Milan Kundera

Contents

9

Bibliographical Note

'The Position of the Afrikaans Writer' was first published in *New Nation*, Johannesburg, September 1967; 'Writers and Writing in the World' is a collation of two lectures delivered at the University of Natal, Pietermaritzburg and Durban, July 1969; 'Mahatma Gandhi Today' was the Gandhi Memorial Lecture delivered at the Phoenix Settlement, Durban, October 1970; 'On Culture and Apartheid' was first published in *Study Project on Christianity in an Apartheid Society*, Spro-cas Publications, No. 1, Johannesburg, 1970; 'English and the Afrikaans Writer' was first published in *Africa*, vol. 3, no. 1, Rhodes University, Grahamstown, 1976; 'Literature and Offence' is a revised version of an article that appeared in *Philosophical Papers*, vol. 5, no. 1, Rhodes University, Grahamstown, 1976; 'After Soweto' was first published in the *Asahi Journal*, Tokyo, 1976; 'Of Slaves and Masters' was first published in the *Argus*, Cape Town, January 1978; 'Mapmakers', a contribution to the theme 'Literature in Disguise' of the Forty-Third International PEN Congress, Stockholm, May 1978, incorporates some material from a talk given at the Cape Town Book Fair, April 1980; 'The Writer in a State of Siege' was a paper read at the Annual General Meeting of the Afrikaans Writers' Guild, Durban, July 1979; 'The Intellectual and His World' was

11

the Graduation Ceremony Address, University of the Witwatersrand, Johannesburg, April 1980; 'Writing Against Silence' was the speech delivered by André Brink on his acceptance of the Martin Luther King Memorial Prize for *A Dry White Season*, London, April 1980; 'The Freedom to Publish' was an address delivered at the Twenty-First Congress of the International Publishers' Association, Stockholm, May 1980; 'Imagining the Real' was a paper that served as the introduction to a discussion on 'Myth in Literature' at the International Writers' Reunion, Lahti, Finland, June 1981; 'The Languages of Culture' was a contribution to the UNESCO Congress on Culture, Mexico City, August 1982; 'Censorship and Literature' first appeared in *Censorship*, a publication issued by the South African Institute of Racial Affairs, Johannesburg, 1982.

Introduction: a Background to Dissidence

I

The essays in this volume have all experienced public exposure before and although they have all been revised, some more extensively than others, each retains the tone of its original context (a talk to students; a contribution to a research project; an academic discussion; a newspaper article aimed at the general public . . .). In selecting them from the large pile of material that has been accumulating in my drawers over the years I did not make any deliberate effort to impose a thematic unity on the whole, but almost spontaneously a central cluster of themes did emerge: the function and responsibility of the writer in society, notably in a state of cultural or moral siege. If there is one conviction that informs all the essays selected for this volume it is that our presence in a world where more and more violence is solving fewer and fewer problems, makes the writer not less, but more, necessary.

For obvious reasons I have concerned myself particularly with the situation in South Africa as it has been developing during the period covered by these essays (1967–1982), and with the position of the Afrikaans writer in this situation.

One of the results of my focus is a measure of overlapping.

In the process of revision I have tried to limit this to a minimum, but a certain amount of repetition remains inevitable because, rather than maim some essays beyond repair, I have opted for the view that different contexts do reveal different nuances in emergent arguments. Approached in this way, some essays can be appreciated more readily as preparatory or exploratory studies leading to others, which also explains my decision to respect chronology. And then, if some things are said several times it is also because I think that, certainly in the South African situation, they not only bear but in fact invite repetition.

II

For an understanding of dissidence within Afrikanerdom, especially in writing, a certain historical perspective may be useful.

When the Dutch East India Company established a refreshment station at the Cape of Good Hope in 1652 there was no ulterior motive aimed at founding a new colony, let alone a new nation. Yet within five years the first Free Burghers were allowed to settle on their own farms, and from that moment a perceptible shift in loyalties became evident: officials continued to look at Holland as *patria*, while the farmers turned to the African soil and began to regard anyone from abroad, including new arrivals from Holland, as foreigners and potential exploiters.

It took four great events during the next three and a half centuries to forge the national consciousness which today determines the concept of Afrikanerdom: and it should be added that *only* on these four occasions was a brief and glorious experience of national unity achieved. In between everything remained very much in a state of flux, characterized by division, hostility, infighting and suspicion.

The first of these moments came in the early years of the

14

eighteenth century, in the joint struggle of Dutch colonists and recently arrived French Huguenots against the oppressive Governor Willem Adriaan van der Stel. In the midst of this general uprising against a tyrannical ruler, a struggle which also hastened the fusion of French with the Dutch dialects spoken at the Cape and thereby paved the way for Afrikaans as a language to emerge, a seventeen-year-old rebel of Stellenbosch, Hendrik Bibault, uttered a defiant statement which can still serve as the motto of the dissident writer:

'I won't go,' he said when the Landdrost (magistrate) ordered him and his unruly companions to disperse. 'I am an Afrikaner, and even if the Landdrost beats me to death or puts me in jail I shall not, and will not, be silent.'

(Bibault was then arrested on a charge of drunkenness; and soon afterwards he was banished from the Cape as the authorities could not tolerate such 'debauches and unruly living'.)

This was the first recorded use of the name *Afrikaner*; and it was peculiarly felicitous in summarizing the priorities of the embryonic new nation.

Afterwards, for nearly a century, while stock farmers moved deep into the interior and staked off their farms so far apart that one would not see a neighbour's smoke anywhere on the horizon, a ruggedly independent race of individuals was forged; and all that bound these intransigents together was the land they lived in, the language they spoke, and the Bible they read.

It was the arrival of the British—a First Occupation in 1795, followed by permanent colonization in 1806—that provided the challenge for a second intimation of national unity. The conflict with Britain resulted, as is well known, in the exodus of thousands of Afrikaners from the Cape Colony in an effort to find a Promised Land elsewhere. Yet the Great Trek, however much it did bring together a large body of Afrikaners and force them into the *laager* existence which preceded full nationhood, also placed severe and continued stress on relationships within the group; in the end it led to a splintering of the Trekkers as they spread across a great tract of land laid bare by the *impis* of Chaka Zulu. And in spite of moments of togetherness in which something of a national 'character' was affirmed, the rest of the century was characterized more by internecine struggle and explosive clashes among many leaders or would-be leaders in the small republics of the Transvaal and the Orange Free State.

It required another overwhelming threat from outside for Afrikaners to be forged into a nation—the Anglo-Boer War (1899–1902), which was the climax of the conflict generated by the discovery of diamonds and gold in the interior from the late 1860s onwards—and the very efforts of Britain in the following years to eradicate Afrikaans as a language and to anglicize the entire South African way of life provoked the reaction which ensured the survival of Afrikanerdom.

But once the threat was removed, with the establishment of Union in 1910, there was yet another lapse into divisions and infighting, aggravated this time by increasing urbanization and the emergence of a large Afrikaner proletariat. Right through two World Wars these divisions persisted, degenerating into civil war in 1914 and coming dangerously close to it again in 1939–45 when some Afrikaners supported General Smuts's war effort while others went underground to sabotage it (with a large, unhappy and uneasy and as yet uncommitted group in the middle).

The fourth moment of national consciousness came with the election victory of the National Party in 1948, although the way for it had already been paved since before the War, with the symbolic convergence of ox-wagons on Pretoria in 1938 to mark the centenary of the Great Trek. In spite of the re-emergence of internal strife during the 1960s the new *laager* of the Afrikaner Establishment this time lasted until the early 1980s, when the old splintering process became overwhelmingly evident once again.

What is to be retained from this is that the widespread notion of 'traditional Afrikaner unity' is based on a false reading of history: strife and inner division within Afrikanerdom has been much more in evidence than unity during the first three centuries of White South African history. It is precisely because today's Afrikaners are so agonizingly aware of what it means to be divided that dissidence in the present circumstances is viewed with such alarm and rage. Apartheid, which defines Afrikaner unity since 1948, needs an image of historicity, preferably of eternity for its success; dissidence exposes it for what it is. And the reaction becomes even more vicious if one takes into account that dissidence, this time, implies a revolt not against some foreign power but against the Afrikaner power base itself. Strife during the nomadic years of the eighteenth century, or in the course of the Great Trek and the history of the short-lived Republics born from it, was invariably based on a clash of personalities, of fiercely independent wills: never was the *raison d'être* of the Afrikaner as a species of humanity dragged into it, which is what is happening now.

Even when the young poet Eugène Marais clashed with President Paul Kruger towards the end of the nineteenth century, what was at stake was two phases of Afrikanerdom—a conservatism vested in Dutch traditions versus a new progressive awareness of Afrikaansness—and it was linked to the universal struggle of morality against corruption. The quarrel did not involve a questioning of the very nature of Afrikanerdom itself (for the simple reason that Afrikanerdom had not yet been defined in ideological terms), which is what the dissidence of our own time is about.

In some important respects the unity confirmed by the elections of 1948 differed from those previous moments in which the Promised Land had been glimpsed. In 1707, in the early nineteenth century, and in 1899–1902 events never led to victory in the historical sense: having won their battle against van der Stel, the burghers withdrew into the interior;

17

in the Great Trek Afrikaners again turned their backs on established 'civilized' territory and departed in search of a mythical utopia which eluded them even in the brief histories of the Boer Republics; the Anglo-Boer War ended in defeat (at least in the short term). But in 1948, for the first time, the Afrikaner came to power in his own country. Earlier Afrikaner governments since 1910 had ruled either in the shadow of the British Empire or, in the 1920s, through coalition. This had made the elusive prize all the more important; and for the newly found power to be threatened from within proved truly traumatic.

Also, the earlier affirmations of emerging nationhood came primarily through struggles *against* value systems regarded as more or less foreign or harmful or both. The victory of 1948 implied the triumph of something Afrikanerdom had come to see as its *own* identity. The problem came when the expression of this identity took the form of the ideology of apartheid. *

In the Afrikaner's evolution towards nationhood there had always been, as should have emerged from the outline above, two major streams of experience: a positive factor, which resided in the Afrikaner's increasing exploration of and identification with Africa; and a negative, in his attempts to assert himself—one of God's chosen people—against others. With the adoption of apartheid as the ideology most suited to the Afrikaner Establishment's image of itself, only the negative factor was affirmed at the expense—no, at the total exclusion—of the positive.

For apartheid to be sanctioned as the definitive characteristic of the Afrikaner Establishment, it had to reach far beyond the domain of politics: it was not simply a political policy 'adopted' as a response to the racial situation in the country but had to be accepted as an extension of an entire

---

* The rise of the ideology of apartheid is discussed with considerable insight in the curate's egg by W. A. de Klerk: *The Puritans in Africa* (London: Collings, 1975).

value system, embracing all the territories of social experience, economics, philosophy, morality and above all religion. The Church itself had to provide the ultimate justification for the ideology.

Even this was not enough: the ideology also attempted to annex the language which had emerged as such a decisive factor in the period of the Anglo-Boer War. Every effort was made to turn Afrikaans into the language of apartheid. This development drew into the arena the writer who realized that to diminish and restrict Afrikaans in this way, as an instrument of the oppressor, went against the very essence of the language. And if ever the Establishment's attempt at hijacking were to succeed, what will be lost to the Afrikaner is not only the future but especially the past: for the language is the living repository of that suppressed but indispensable positive aspect of the Afrikaner's experience—that is, of everything lived through in the hard process of learning not only to survive *in* this continent but to survive as *part* of it: part of its blood and flesh and bones and guts, part of its deep and awful rhythms.

If the Afrikaner dissident today encounters such a vicious reaction from the Establishment, it is because he is regarded as a traitor to everything Afrikanerdom stands for (since apartheid has usurped for itself that definition)—whereas, in fact, the dissident is fighting to assert the most positive and creative aspects of his heritage, which are involved with that experience of Africa he shares with other Africans.

In summary, apartheid, as I see it, denies what is best in the Afrikaner himself. It reveals only that side of him which is characterized by fear, by suspicion, by uncertainty, hence by arrogance, meanness, narrowmindedness, pighead-edness. What it denies is the Afrikaner's reverence for life, his romanticism, his sense of the mystical, his deep attach-ment to the earth, his generosity, his compassion.

The eventual destruction of apartheid *need* not automatically imply the disappearance of the Afrikaner himself: only the eradication of his negative side. But if he does not put things right himself, if he continues to assert only his negative image, he will inevitably lose all. The dissident writer knows this, and appreciates the tragic possibilities inherent in the situation: consequently his struggle is not just *against* what is evil in the Afrikaner, but *for* what he perceives to be his potential for good. In other words, it is not just a struggle aimed at the liberation of blacks from oppression by whites, but also a struggle for the liberation of the Afrikaner from the ideology in which he has come to negate his better self. The dissident struggles in the name of what the Afrikaner could and should have become in the light of his own history, had he not allowed adversity (both real and imaginary) to narrow down his horizon to the small hard facts of mere physical survival.

III

It is tricky to talk about Afrikaner dissidence prior to 1910; even, strictly speaking, prior to 1948, because during that early history dissidence meant rebellion against established authorities from outside, not the Afrikaner Establishment itself. Even so, some significant aspects of present-day dissidence can be illuminated by looking at the pioneering days when the positive aspects of Afrikanerdom mentioned above had not yet been submerged.

What strikes one immediately is how the early dissidents, most of them rather picaresque figures, based their revolt against authorities on a total identification with the African continent: almost a century after Bibault's generation, the burghers of Graaff Reinet and Swellendam proclaimed the independence of their two minuscule village-republics in the face of the foreign invader who, they said, knew nothing about Africa. (At the same time, charmingly, those burghers felt themselves inspired by the French Revolution and went so far as to start addressing each other as *citoyen* and *citoyenne!*) In the early years of the nineteenth century the archetype of the Afrikaner rebel was the almost legendary Coenraad de Buys, outlaw and fugitive, who lived across the border of the Colony with his black wife and deliberately and extravagantly broke all the colonial laws that came in his way. His contemporary, Frederik Bezuidenhout, also reported to be living with a dark-skinned wife, defied British authority so audaciously that a contingent of soldiers was eventually sent to haul him to court: when he was shot dead, the farmers of the Eastern Frontier rose up in arms and tried to persuade the black chief Ngqika to join them. This aborted rebellion of Slagtersnek became one of the prime causes of the Great Trek.

The very first of the Trekkers, Louis Trichardt, was himself a rather off-beat individual who allegedly smuggled guns to the Xhosas for years before he loaded his wagon; at the time most of his closest neighbours and friends were, in fact, black.

Within the context of their time these colourful characters—and there were many others—may appear 'merely' picaresque in appearance. But what they did establish was a complete identification with Africa and her indigenous peoples, which would serve as an example to the infinitely more sophisticated dissidents of our time. If the modern Afrikaner dissident sets himself up against the authorities of 'his own people', it is because he sees an act of betrayal in the course these people have chosen: a course leading towards the very abuses which, in the distant past, used to characterize the 'foreign oppressor'.

The oneness with Africa which inspires the latterday rebel, and his solidarity with oppressed blacks, is radically different from the philanthropic sentiments of white Liberals, the *noblesse de robe* who, like those of Racine's time, can afford to clash with authority because they are basically *protected* by it. Even that crabby and often crooked

21

old rascal, Paul Kruger, acquired a touch of grandeur in his resistance to Britain because what he was fundamentally inspired by was his identification with this land, this Africa. This was the sentiment that informed those noble words spoken as early as 1881:

'With confidence we expose our cause to the whole world. Whether we triumph or die freedom will rise in Africa like the sun from the morning clouds.'

It is no coincidence that these words were quoted many years later by Bram Fischer when he was sentenced to life imprisonment: for Fischer became another great example of Afrikaner dissidence (cf. 'Mahatma Gandhi Today'). While 'his own people' accused him of aligning himself with the enemy he was really demonstrating that sense of justice and liberty and that identification with Africa which had been running in the river bed of true Afrikanerdom for centuries: a sense inspired by a history, shared with black Africans, of a tribal past, of the peasant's closeness to the earth, and of being exploited by 'others' from 'elsewhere'.

Another inspiring name in the heroes' gallery of Afrikaner dissidence is the Rev. Beyers Naudé who has been living, for the past five years , under banning orders and who has lent a specifically Christian dimension to resistance against oppression. (It comes as no surprise that the influential young religious leader Dr Alan Boesak also mentions Naudé as the greatest inspiration of his life.) But between Fischer and Naudé something interesting has happened. At the time of Fischer's revolt Afrikanerdom found it possible to ostracize him utterly. Beyers Naudé on the other hand, hounded, harassed and persecuted as he has been ever since he turned against the secret Broederbond which is the guardian of ideology in the National Party, has retained so much sympathy within the *laager* and has so many admirers among young Afrikaners that his ostracism can never be complete.

This explains why the next generation, the writers known

as the Sestigers, were able to go yet another step further: condemned by the Establishment they nevertheless evoked such a wave of sympathy and enthusiasm among young readers that to a large extent their rejection by the powers that be rebounded on the authorities themselves.

IV

Ever since the First Afrikaans Language Movement started in 1875 there have been dissident writers in various forms and guises. The champions of the language were themselves dissidents within the larger context of 'Dutch' South Africa, both in the Cape Colony and the Transvaal: their most formidable opponents were the members of the Dutch Reformed Church Synod who saw in the young language a threat to all that was venerable and 'Christian' in Church tradition. But of course, within the framework of the emerging Afrikaner nation, these writers were all fervent patriots living up to Durrell's bleak description of puritanism: 'A puritan culture's conception of art is of something which will endorse its morality and flatter its patriotism . . . '

Which means that in those early years, until about 1920, one should not look for dissidence on the obvious, political level, but elsewhere: in Eugène Marais's evocation of the Sān ('Bushman') world in his best poems at a time when poetry seldom went beyond doggerel, or in his keen, inquisitive, scientific and pseudo-scientific explorations of the life of baboons and termites at a time when such undertakings were regarded as 'anti-Christian'; in the poet Leipoldt's compassion for all the innocent victims of war when no more than the narrowest chauvinism was expected of him; or in his use of material from medieval Catholicism in a play written in a society of extremist Calvinists; or in his flirtations with Buddhism and his provocative statements on all matters regarded by his contemporaries as taboo, ranging from

23

substituting wine for milk as a beverage for young children to concepts of nationalism and the occult.

In the 1920s a few poets became more outspoken, notably Toon van den Heever, whose incisive cynicism in rejecting all conventional Afrikaner values from Calvinism to decorum in love riled his contemporaries. The first persistent questioners of the system, the generation of Van Wyk Louw, made their appearance in the 1930s and opened the windows of Afrikaans literature to the outside world: the philosophies of Schopenhauer, of Nietzsche, of Hegel (with a sound dose of *Mein Kampf* thrown in for good measure) invaded Afrikaans poetry; sexual love, including homosexual love, was introduced as a theme; above all, this generation rejected the notion of the poet as mouthpiece of his people and insisted on the primacy of the individual's perception and experience of the world. But if they brought about the emancipation of Afrikaans poetry and the breaking of the shackles of colonialism, their explorations seldom went beyond the rather cautious boundaries defined by notions like 'loyal resistance' and 'liberal nationalism'. Only in his later work did Van Wyk Louw feel free to castigate un-remittingly—yet always with comprehension and com-passion—his 'own people'. If this generation incurred the wrath of their Afrikaans contemporaries it was not for writing dissident verse but for writing what to the *volk*, the 'people', appeared abstruse, incomprehensible, obscure. Yet on at least one occasion of tremendous symbolic significance Van Wyk Louw did collide openly with the Establishment. In 1938 he had written a patriotic play for the centenary festival of the Great Trek in which he found the *raîson d'être* of Afrikanerdom in the suffering of his people throughout history: true to the demands of the time he had provided exactly what was expected of a 'national' poet. But when he was commissioned to write another play for the Republic Festival in 1966, the new work, instead of extolling the virtues of the *volk* and glorifying their history, turned out to be a profound examination of the very nature of nationhood. Rather than affirming generally accepted values Louw posed an initial question: 'What is a nation?'— and took it from there, leading not to answers but only to more and more new questions. This incurred the wrath of the redoubtable prime minister, Dr Verwoerd, who in his major Republic Day speech delivered a devastating attack on Louw in particular and writers in general. What a pity Louw refused to reply ('How can a whale fight against an elephant?' asked the poet D. J. Opperman on his behalf). But his silence was probably eloquent enough.

Only with the generation of the 1940s can Afrikaans poetry be said really to approach a dimension of overt political dissidence: in the first hesitant questions posed by the coloured poet S. V. Petersen (later to be overtaken by the eloquent and angry lyricism of Adam Small), and especially by D. J. Opperman, the first Afrikaans poet openly to explore and expose the racial complexities of South Africa and to reveal in unforgettable and concrete imagery the essential humanity of all who inhabit this land, be they black, or brown, or white. In the mid-1950s, his short poem 'Kersliedjie' ('Christmas Carol') caused an uproar within the Establishment through its evocation of Christ born as a brown baby in the coloured ghetto of District Six in Cape Town. In 'Staking op die suikerplantasie' ('Strike on the Sugar Cane Plantation') Opperman disturbed the time-honoured equation of White and Black with Good and Evil by revealing the elements of evil and chaos within white civilization itself; in 'Springbokke' he offered an apocalyptic vision of Afrikanerdom stampeding into the sea like a crazed herd of springbok; in countless poems he affirmed the essential oneness of all people irrespective of colour—always transcending the purely political to a level of visionary intensity.

In the 1950s Opperman was joined by Peter Blum, a strange comet that briefly and dazzlingly streaked through our southern skies: born in Trieste and arriving at the Cape as a student with no knowledge of Afrikaans, he soon learned the language and became one of its most illustrious poets (in two thin volumes only: afterwards he packed his belongings and emigrated). More than any of his predecessors, Blum exposed the Afrikaner's tenuous hold on the land and viewed him against a background of the apocalypse, whether with a bang or a whimper.

V

The generation of the Sestigers broadened the base of contestation in Afrikaans literature. As their work is constantly referred to in the essays of this volume, a brief indication of the framework of their renewal and the general development of the movement should suffice here.

It was a movement—inasmuch as the work of a small group of such widely divergent temperaments and talents can be termed a movement—with purely literary origins, starting as a revolt against hackneyed themes and outworn structures in Afrikaans fiction. But because so much of it was European in inspiration—which appealed immensely to younger readers but came as a cultural shock to the Establishment and all its agencies—the iconoclastic ardour of these writers soon caused them to collide head-on with most of the established religious and moral values of 'traditional' Afrikanerdom. As a result, even though most of this early work had no overt political slant, its implications were political; and especially in the work of the 'father' of the movement, Jan Rabie (*Ons, die Afgod* (*We, the Idol*); and his *Bolandia* cycle of novels on the shared history of whites and coloureds) political issues were articulated explicitly. The vehemence of the cultural collision and the extent of its reverberations throughout Afrikanerdom cannot be fully understood from the outside unless the real horror at the thought of anyone leaving the *laager* is appreciated.

Because of the political dimension within which the work of the new generation operated, it was only a matter of time before the writers involved would embark on an exploration of the political consequences of their early interest in human relationships. Towards the end of the 1960s there was a brief but fierce clash between two groups of Sestigers in the magazine *Kol* (*Spot*): the first, in which writers like Etienne Leroux and Chris Barnard were prominent, championed the cause of *l'art pur;* Jan Rabie, Breyten Breytenbach and I insisted on the need for literature to take arms within and against the socio-political realities of South Africa. Although we all rejected the notion of facile and superficial forms of social realism, agitprop or propaganda, we believed very strongly that, given the society we worked in, literature could only be vital by exploring openly the issues involved within that society: even silence and non-commitment, we felt, implied a political stance. In some circles this battle still rages on today; but it is significant that most of the key figures among the Sestigers, including those who had initially argued very strongly against commitment, have in the course of the 1970s broadened the scope of their writing to include the contemporary South African scene. In *Magersfontein, o Magersfontein* Etienne Leroux presents a grotesquely new view of one of Afrikanerdom's sacred events, the Battle of Magersfontein in the Anglo-Boer War, in the form of a film team's efforts to reconstruct the original: it inevitably ends in an apocalyptic Flood. The short story writer Abraham de Vries in recent work has provided a number of disconcerting glimpses of people torn asunder in an apartheid society. In *Donderdag of Woensdag* (*Thursday or Wednesday*) John Miles brilliantly exploits the form of the thriller—the kidnapping of a statesman in whom even the most inexperienced reader will recognize the previous prime minister John Balthazar Vorster—to provide a devastating satire of South African mores. Even an essentially apolitical writer like Karel Schoeman has offered, notably in *The*

Promised Land, chilling views of the results of Afrikaner intransigence. Elsa Joubert, who has been profoundly fascinated by Africa since her earliest work, caused a furore in Afrikaner circles with her *Poppie Nongena*, the heartrendingly sincere account of a simple black woman's efforts to find a place she can call her own: it would not be an overstatement to say that, in this fictionalized biography, Elsa Joubert has done for Afrikaners what Paton's *Cry the Beloved Country* did for white readers in general three decades earlier. As I indicated in the Postscript to 'Culture and Apartheid', works like these prove that the cultural schizophrenia experienced by Sestigers who, in their early work, could not reconcile their cosmopolitan outlook with the *laager* mentality of Afrikanerdom, finally resolved the conflicts within themselves by 'coming home' to Africa in the fullest sense of the word.

One should not deduce from this that Afrikaans literature is flourishing. On the contrary. Censorship and various forms of harassment during the 1970s have so intimidated writers that almost no new Afrikaans novelist of any importance has appeared on the scene in the past decade. (Poets, on the other hand, have published abundantly, a phenomenon discussed elsewhere in this volume.) The writers mentioned above had already established themselves during the 1960s, which made it more difficult for the authorities to silence them. The enormous resonance their work has found among young Afrikaans readers inhibits more stringent measures taken against them. At the same time no one should underestimate the obstacles placed in the way of a writer who decides to speak out against the South African Government. The active war of intimidation waged by the Security Police and others against him, looms large and real in the daily life and even in the most private experience of such a writer. And the constant threat of being cut off from his readers—which is much easier to effect within a small language like Afrikaans than in one of the

28

major languages of the world—creates in the writer a particular agony. It is from this vulnerability that is derived so much of the writer's awareness of his function in a restricted society and his responsibility towards his world, which has inspired the majority of the essays in this volume.

VI

I was born on a bench in the Luxembourg Gardens in Paris, in the early spring of 1960.

I had been born earlier too, of course; and after that cool bright spring morning in Paris I experienced several other births as well, some easy, some traumatic, but none quite so decisive as that one. In the European autumn of the previous year I had arrived in Paris to embark on postgraduate research in comparative literature. I learned much about literature during the two years I was to spend at the Sorbonne, but more about the world, about life, about myself. For more than twenty years I had led a tranquil, almost uneventful life in a succession of small South African villages, all of them predominantly Afrikaans, all of them extremely conservative, all of them steeped in an almost Old Testament world of Calvinist rigorism. On the farms where I had spent many of my childhood holidays I had played together with the other boys, black and white, with no second thoughts about our different shades of brown or pink. Just as unquestioningly I later accepted the gradual differentiation of my world, the fact that colour determined the structure of society. Race and class were identical; and since there was simply no possibility of encountering a black person in any role other than that of servant or labourer, questions about 'humanity' never entered the picture. The difference between the races, I believed, like all my contemporaries, had been ordained by God and was the result of the curse on the children of Canaan and the confusion of Babel. After school I went to Potchefstroom

University, a small institution and a bastion of Calvinism. There were no black students, of course; in my experience they did not exist. One could spend a lifetime in South Africa in those years, as many still do, living so exclusively within one of the many totally segregated microcosms that exist side by side in the country, without ever having contact—except on the most superficial level—with others. You hardly knew they existed. If other people did exist, they were *they*: the black masses; the other. At most, they could be won over to the Christian cause through missionary work, which might minimize the threat they posed to white civilization. No more.

And yet, inevitably, there were small things, almost imperceptible when they happened, but accumulating all the time, a subterranean, subconscious presence, ready to emerge when one would eventually have matured sufficiently to acknowledge them. My father was a magistrate. Many afternoons of my childhood I huddled in a back corner of the courtroom to stare and listen, in awe, to the cases brought before him. Most stemmed from a world so remote from my own that they never penetrated my consciousness. Such things happened to black people; they didn't really concern me. Except that a deeply rooted respect was born in me, not just for the law, which my father represented, but for justice, which he incarnated. That people can wrong one another, and that blacks are often wronged, was notched deeply into my mind, as was the relief at knowing that redress for wrongs was possible, certainly when it depended on my father.

Even so, what happened in the courtroom happened at second hand: not crime itself, but the rumour and report of crime. But one day a black man came to our house, streaming with blood, a sickening sight. He had been beaten by his master, he said; and then he had gone to the police to complain and they had beaten him some more. Now he had come to us for help. My father wasn't there just then, but

30

when he came home he did what I had known he would. He used his authority to make sure the man's complaint would be heard.

While I was at university a young black boy who had been working in the garden of friends absconded. He was hunted down and brought back, and taken into the garage, and beaten nearly to death. His master was one of the kindest and most affable people I have ever known. The boy had done wrong to run away, of course. But what struck me was the realization that he'd never been given any choice about where or how he wanted to work. He'd been 'booked' into the master's service and that was that. The beating had been terrible enough; but this was worse. He had had no choice.

One day a leading black academic, one of the most learned and wise of men, the late Professor Z. K. Matthews, visited our university and addressed the students. The hall overflowed. He was received with great enthusiasm, and for a long time afterwards some of us continued to discuss the event. Not the address so much, although that in itself had been remarkable; but the fact that, for the first time in our protected lives, we had encountered a black man who was not a labourer or a servant.

In 1955 the 60,000 black inhabitants of Sophiatown, outside Johannesburg, were forcibly evicted from their homes and removed, at gunpoint, to another place of abode, as the area was required for white housing. The Afrikaans newspapers, the only ones we read at university, called it a great step forward, both socially and politically. Soon afterwards Father Trevor Huddleston published his book on the events which had culminated in that shameful act. It made an indelible impression on me: it was the first time someone had, at such length, and in such detail, explained 'the other side' to me. I fought against the revelations of *Naught for Your Comfort* all the way; on every page of my battered copy, when I leaf through it today, I find my angry comments, debating him, querying him, attacking him. But he wore me down. Even though I would not concede it at the time—and my conservative surroundings made it easy not to concede—Father Huddleston had opened my eyes to something I hadn't realized before.

This was the frame of mind in which I went to Paris in 1959, sure of my convictions, comfortable in my chauvinism, bolstered by my religious persuasion: though with some uneasy, nagging doubt very deep down. But Paris was not Potchefstroom. After seven years at university, in a small relaxed place where everyone knew everybody else, where all reactions, including cautious rebellion, were predictable and containable, suddenly I found myself in that great metropolis where every single thing I had always taken for granted now had to be tested, explored, validated—or rejected.

The simple experience of sitting down for a meal in a student restaurant and finding blacks at the same table, came as a shock. What had previously been so impossible that it had never even crossed the threshold of the thinkable, was now happening as a matter of course. To discover that many of my new black colleagues were able to hold their own in conversations about literature, philosophy, politics and a thousand other subjects, and that in fact they often had read much more, and knew much more, than I did, left me in an almost perpetual daze.

Only a few months after my arrival in Paris came the news of Sharpeville where scores of people demonstrating peacefully against the pass laws, were shot dead by the police. For days on end it seemed as if the whole country would be sinking. Being so far away from it all made the picture that much more agonizingly clear. All the trivialities that tend to obscure the day-by-day evolution of a situation when one finds oneself in the thick of it, were removed to expose the outlines as relentlessly as the backbone of a fish. My people, it seemed, were going down. I felt a gut reaction to hurry back and sink with them. But it was ridiculous, of course. And the terrible thing I had to come to terms with on that clear spring morning in the Luxembourg Gardens was this: that if this were really the apocalypse, if 'my people' were really sinking—then it was their own fault, the inevitable retribution for what they themselves had done and had allowed to be done; and as in the distant past I felt myself crouching at the back of a dimly lit courtroom, watching the inexorable wheels of justice turning, turning, grinding, exceedingly small.

The enormity of the experience was such that I could not immediately come to terms with it. What had really happened, it now seems to me, is that the two years I spent in Paris was time enough to break down all my previously held certainties and convictions; but not enough for a new and positive set of possibilities to emerge from the rubble. At that stage, literature to me was not so much a weapon of attack or a refuge as a means of probing the new emergent meanings in myself. And this process could only take place in interaction with the society whose structures I had begun to doubt.

When the early novels of my Sestiger phase caused the reaction they did—violent condemnation from the Establishment; enthusiasm from the younger generation—there was both exhilaration and agony in the experience. Exhilaration because writing had become such an adventurous form of communicating with a society in a state of agitation; agony because I had to come to terms with the realities of harassment and ostracism in relation to people and institutions to which I had previously been close.

After a few years the initial fervour of the Sestigers began to wane: most of our immediate battles had been gained. And they had taken a certain toll, too: a weariness caused by the discovery that one had been struggling for a few peripheral liberties which, everywhere else in the free world, were already taken for granted by writers. Our goals were in fact their starting points. That, at least, was what it seemed like in the mid-1960s: because we were still wary of admitting, even to ourselves, that in a totally politicized society like South Africa, we had simply not yet gone far enough. Our very 'literariness' was beginning to turn into our own worst enemy.

At the end of 1967 I left for Paris again—this time with the aim of investigating the possibilities of settling in France permanently. I spent the year of 1968 mainly in Paris, in very close contact with the poet Breyten Breytenbach who had been living there in voluntary exile ever since his marriage to a Vietnamese girl some years before.* I had been back on visits to Paris several times before that: but 1968 was, understandably, different.

No need to dwell on the new birth that happened in myself. I had already begun to introduce a political dimension in my work by then, specifically in a novel (*The Saboteurs*) which remained unpublished. But the experience of being, once again, remote from South Africa and able to achieve a new clarity and inevitability of vision, brought to me the sense of direction I had lacked before. It immediately involved my position in Paris, too. It is a city I love above all others; whenever I set foot in France, I feel revived, refreshed, inspired; the romantic love-affair I have been involved in with this city will last a lifetime. Some of my best friends lived there at the time. And yet I could not stay on. If the student revolt of 1968 brought into focus one issue above all others, surely it was the relationship of the individual with his society, and his need to assume responsibility within that society.

To stay on in Paris would imply that literature, to me, had become a luxury to be indulged in, an intriguing diversion. If, on the other hand, writing was as important to me as I knew it was, it could be done in one place only: in the midst of that society to which I had now come to acknowledge my

* Having returned to South Africa, Breytenbach was jailed and then suddenly released in early December 1982. He is now resident in Paris again.

profound and agonizing commitment. Returning to South Africa meant one thing: that writing had become an indispensable dimension of my life; and that I was prepared to assume full responsibility for every word I would write in future.

Ever since my return I have been involved, and ever more deeply involved, in what is happening in this country. I have made enemies; I have made wonderful new friends. I cherish especially those friendships across the artificial barriers of race, which have grown and deepened over the years. It has not been easy. Every step of the way has been a struggle: not just against the visible obstacles and adversaries in my way, the structures of apartheid and its deadly ramifications, but against the invisible forces acting in the dark against the writer—forces many Afrikaners do not know about, because they refuse to accept that 'their own people' could stoop to such strategies. There lies a peculiar satisfaction in countering the tactics of secrecy with exposure: the dark fears nothing quite so much as light. This in itself is a justification for writing, and for continuing to write.

I am here because I *want* to be here, because in my innermost self I know I *must* be here: because I love this land with a deep and terrible love: because not being here would be spiritual death.

In the fullest sense of the word this is an experience of being *in situation*. Which is something radically different from 'being within the system'! In fact, only by being not only in situation but, if it is at all possible, *sur place*, can one make sure that the system is exposed, countered and eventually shattered: in the name of that truth all writers go in search of, that freedom which can only be born from the rebellion against unfreedom, and that justice of which as a barefoot boy I caught a glimpse that can never fade—provided one commit oneself unconditionally to the need to state it, and restate it, and state it again, and again, and forever.

The Position
of the Afrikaans Writer

(1967)

If the position of the English writer in South Africa is unenviable, it is at least unequivocal: his work is banned. Not all of it, of course, but if the case of Nadine Gordimer can be regarded as indicative, certainly the most accomplished, the most *effective* work by an English writer is liable to be banned. At the very least there are no qualms in the minds of the authorities about banning English works: these writers are traditionally regarded as enemies of the Afrikaner—so what else can be expected of them? The Afrikaans writer, on the other hand, still has the uneasy knowledge that although the authorities loathe his guts, no official action has been taken against an Afrikaans book (yet). But does that imply that the position of the Afrikaans writer is more safe and secure than that of his black, brown or white compatriots writing in English? The matter is not so simple.

Even though an English writer may be denied a local market he is still affiliated, through language and culture, to a large Anglo-Saxon world in which he is allowed to exercise his true function as a writer. On the other hand one should have no illusions about the spiritual agony of a writer whose works are kept away from the people for whom he has written in the first place: Nadine Gordimer's banned *The Late Bourgeois World* should primarily be read by South Africans.

The Afrikaans writer has so far been allowed to publish his work in his own country—or *some* of his work, for the public is not aware, I think, of the formidable and growing power of pre-publication censorship applied by most of the larger publishing firms with political affiliations. I think—I hope— that no really good Afrikaans novel will ultimately fail to find a local publisher; but that is really only the beginning of the struggle, which is basically a struggle against lies and the denial of justice.

From one point of view it seems unnecessary to pay too much attention to some of these 'organizations' acting in the name of Christianity or Nationalism or, preferably, both: surely they are no more than the pathetic and desperate crusades of angry old men? In this brand of conservatism, it may be argued, it is simply the immemorial conflict between old and young which is revealed with particular violence and bitterness. These self-appointed leaders invoke the magic and mythical *volk* as the mainspring of their fulminations, the *raison d'être* of their sound and fury—but is the *volk* really concerned with it? Or are most people simply amused by Christian Cultural Action Congresses and other gatherings which reveal very little Christian love and only a distorted sense of culture?

If the resistance against younger Afrikaans writing was confined to small men and little groups it would, indeed, have been unnecessary to dwell too long on it. But these actions appear as the mere symptoms of a much deeper problem, and they are intimately linked with the un-precedented strife and infighting and backbiting rocking Afrikanerdom at the moment—clashing political ambitions, turmoil in the Churches, cultural and industrial conflict, etc.

Politically, the Afrikaner is in power. During the first half of the century the mere struggle to gain that power kept Afrikaans-speaking people together; an Afrikaner was automatically a supporter of the Party and a member of one of the three 'Sister Churches' (even though these weird Sisters didn't always reveal much brotherly love). Once political supremacy had been achieved, however, the natural differences characteristic of all societies inevitably began to assert themselves. Unfortunately this is happening at a moment when South Africa is particularly vulnerable in the eyes of the world: if Afrikanerdom crumbles, the entire edifice of our society, it is argued, may be ruined. That is why those in control of State, Church or organized culture insist that the present is no time ' to reason why', but simply 'to do or die', which accounts for the extraordinary vehemence of their reactions.

In this society the Afrikaans writer occupies a strange and important place. It is not yet a century since the First Language Movement began to promote Afrikaans as a language; the first Afrikaans poem of some literary merit was written a mere sixty years ago. In other words, in the minds of probably the majority of Afrikaners, the writer is still supposed to exercise the function he had in a society at the very beginning of its evolution. He is supposed to encourage the solidarity of his people and to promote their group identity—as was expected of Homer or the narrators of the *Nibelungenlied*, of Afrikaner pioneers, or of the writers of Soviet Russia or Red China. In the meantime, however, the world has changed utterly and within the international cultural society the writer, including the Afrikaner, has a different function altogether. Both artist and scientist belong, as Goethe said two centuries ago, to humanity as a whole. In spite of the vicissitudes in the life of a nation it is the duty of the writer to probe beneath the surface, to pose dangerous questions, to discover essential human truths.

Of course this may turn the writer into the notorious 'gadfly of society'; of course this makes him obnoxious to the conscience of the political leader who works with common denominators rather than with individuals: but that is his duty. Without that, society stagnates.

Now this is exactly the function of which our authorities wish to deprive Afrikaans writers, not realizing that the result would be that blind stampede of springboks into the sea in search of salt evoked in Opperman's moving poem, 'Springbokke'. When Etienne Leroux dares to reveal some of the flaws and follies of South African society in *Seven Days at the Silbersteins* all possible pretexts from the ethical to the linguistic are used in an effort to discredit his work. If younger writers dare suggest that morality involves more than 'Yes, Baas', marriage, and family prayers, or that love is a metaphysical experience transcending the adoration of a *princesse lointaine* or some amorous gropings in a farmhouse, or that modern society is urbanized and involves rather more than the traditional afflictions of farmers, or that politics has a larger spectrum than Nationalism, our works are proscribed and their authors ostracized. And the onslaught is not restricted to the rantings of self-appointed popes of morality, or to an avalanche of letters to the press, but extends to the radio (by refusing younger writers any opportunity of explaining their views), to schools (by forbidding children to read younger writers), to churches (by intimidating printers and publishers). An insidious campaign against liberal trends in younger writers strives to persuade the nation that they are also heralds of communism—and in this way a climate is slowly created in which, it is hoped, this young, flourishing literature can be stifled.

It is all so unnecessary. A book which fails in its exploration of significant patterns in society and in the relationships of individuals, is doomed to die—whether attacked by the puritans or not; and a truly good book will inevitably survive, in spite of all attempts to kill it, just as *Madame Bovary* survived, or, in our time, *Doctor Zhivago*.

The danger is that once a climate is created in which Afrikaans works can be banned as easily as those in English, the Afrikaans writer may be forced to find other markets, like

Pasternak: for the writer does not only write, but writes to be read. The English writer banned in South Africa still lives on in an English cultural tradition abroad, however painful the silence imposed on him at home: the Afrikaner may be uprooted more completely. If he is good enough, he will survive. But the price will be paid by his country. And it is a price this young society cannot afford. Already a danger point is drawing near. And if our culture is to flourish—if it is to survive at all—South Africa will have to make room for gadflies and bees in its smug little garden.

Writers and Writing
in the World

(1969)

Writers and their writing exist in the world: even the most private poem, written for the poet's personal enjoyment and hidden in his bottom drawer, presupposes a reader. Without functioning within a process of communication, it remains only partially realized.

But does this mean that the literary work is inevitably directed towards the fulfilment of some social function? Can it be taken for granted that the writer and his work can count on a form of social effect?

I

To explore this, one should of course be careful to distinguish between the nature of a work and its possible effect: there is a wide difference between what the work *is* and what it *does*—or what can be done with or to it. Notre-Dame in Paris, has, among other things, been used as a stable, a church, a court of law and a sanctuary for criminals and beggars: but it remains, in the final analysis, a *building*. As with buildings, literature has been used and abused in many ways—by authors and readers alike. Books have been used to flatter tyrants or to contribute to their fall; to prove theories

41

or disprove them; to fight sinful lust or to stimulate the reader's sexuality; to praise women or to hurl abuse at them; they have been used to inspire men, to convey beauty, to kindle barbecue fires or to prop up rickety shelves.

But the uses to which books have been put need not have anything to do with the function implicit in literature. A specific example: so many critics have attacked the Sestigers on the grounds that their books might impair the morals of youthful readers. None of these vociferous critics seems to blame the Bible for the fact that many passages and chapters in it are constantly used by adolescents for sexual titillation. Even a book written with the noblest of intentions can be misused by malicious or idiotic or even well-meaning readers.

But this should not lead us into another pitfall: that, namely, of the 'author's intention'. Authors' intentions are erratic and unpredictable and most unreliable. T. S. Eliot once explained, perhaps with the wisdom of hindsight, that he had intended *Murder in the Cathedral* as anti-Nazi propaganda: it is to be doubted whether any reader would have guessed this, had Eliot not mentioned it himself. (Incidentally, this may be the case with several works in Afrikaans as well: novels and poems express their social comment in cryptic symbols which, in a good work, become important in their own right but, in a bad work, degenerate into escapism.) Yet whether or not Eliot's play is anti-Nazi has nothing to do with the fact that it is an outstanding work of art.

And there are numerous other examples. *Don Quixote* was originally written as a devastating comment on the tradition of picaresque novels and on the Spanish conquistadores but its lasting greatness has little to do with the impulses which prompted its writing in the first place.

The greatest novel in nineteenth-century Dutch literature, Multatuli's *Max Havelaar*, was written to expose the intolerable conditions in the East Indies: the book ends with a personal, passionate plea to the Prince of Orange himself. The book was an enormous success: but everybody was so moved by the characters in their own right that no one paid any attention to the plight of the Javanese.

There are many modern examples, too: probably no other playwright in our century has been more 'committed' than Brecht: yet we have the word of a leading producer that when pure fantasy is required in Polish theatre, it is Brecht who is performed. At the same time that 'absurd' classic of the modern stage, *Waiting for Godot*, has been performed in Poland as the epitome of *théâtre engagé*: because there the waiting of Estragon and Vladimir could be interpreted politically as the waiting of the inmates of Auschwitz.

There is another example of the latter sort: when Pasternak was first confronted with official condemnation, he retired into silence. When he emerged, it was to publish the purest lyrical poetry. And yet these poems were interpreted as political provocation: because to write lyrical verse in a social context where political commitment or flattery of the system is not only expected but required, amounts to a challenge in itself. And so we are back where we started: i.e., the author's intentions may be almost universally regarded as irrelevant for the eventual quality of his work.

Even so, one cannot deny that much of the persuasive passion of *Don Quixote* or the *Max Havelaar* derives precisely from the anger of a committed author, and that without that flame no mind would have been set alight by those works. Similarly, the agony and rage of James Baldwin or LeRoi Jones determine much of the compelling quality of their writing: it is as if the violence of their commitment is enhanced within the dimensions of their work.

This happens, too, in Nadine Gordimer's *The Late Bourgeois World*, but not in *An Occasion for Loving*. And it is interesting to note that *The Late Bourgeois World* is banned in South Africa whereas *An Occasion for Loving* is not, although the latter, with its theme of love-across-the-colour-bar, may seem much more 'inflammable' in the South African context than the first. But its flame is short-lived, while that of *The Late Bourgeois World* transcends the original anger and becomes, in the process, more 'dangerous'—which, in literature, often appears to be synonymous with 'great'.

II

What we have found so far, is that although a writer's personal intention may have little to do with the success of his work, the *quality* of his anger may enlarge the scope of his work. And obviously the quality of his anger will be related, however tenuously, to the causes of that anger: the tantrum of a child who has been refused a sweet may be explosive in its own right but is much more restricted in its 'human scope' than the rage of a person fighting for justice in the face of suffering. I shall in due course explore more fully the meanings I attach to this vague and over-exposed term 'human scope'. For the moment, what requires our attention is an acknowledgement of the fact that, in turning to the nature and sources of anger, we have shifted our focus from the *work* to the *writer*. And although both act as agents in the world, the range of their possible functions should not be confused.

I have referred to Pasternak and to the political weight attached even to his utterly non-political poems. Of course he exerted an even greater influence on the world at large through *Doctor Zhivago*. And yet it remains true that thousands, perhaps millions of people in the West were moved by Pasternak's 'stand', by what he represented, even though they may never have read his book. Just as millions have been inspired by those other Russian dissidents, Sinyavsky and Daniel, even though most know nothing whatsoever about their work.

We admire them because they exemplify resistance to oppression; because in them something courageous has survived, not for them alone, but for all people.

On a much, much smaller scale the same phenomenon has become evident in South Africa with the advent of the Sestigers. Through their resistance to traditional pressures within their puritanical society and their revolt against obsolescence in letters and ethics, the impact of their renewal went far beyond the frontiers of literature. Their work became, first, a cultural, then a political phenomenon. Social attitudes within Afrikanerdom are assessed, even today, on the basis of whether a person is 'for' or 'against' the Sestigers. And this applies as much to people who have read their work as to a multitude who haven't. The ripple effect has even gone beyond Afrikanerdom itself: to many English speakers in the country and, even more significantly, to a large number of coloureds and blacks (who have never read a word of the Sestigers) this work has come to signify a revolt against an entire oppressive system. In the process, the Sestigers have acquired an importance out of all proportion to what they have actually achieved in terms of literature.

I am not trying to denigrate what has been written by these writers. Some outstanding work has, in fact, been produced; and Afrikaans letters after Breytenbach and Etienne Leroux, to name but two, can never be quite the same as before. But what concerns me most at the moment is that the peculiar social function fulfilled by (or forced on?) writers of the Sestiger generation also imposes an enormous social, moral and political responsibility on us all.

Whether we like it or not, in our particular situation, in *this* country, we have assumed, through what we have written, a responsibility not only to our métier but also, by implication, to every individual who reacts to our words.

45

III

Can the writer be described as a Pippa passing through the world, singing a song that alters something, and creates something, in each listener who hears it? Perhaps it would do greater justice to his function to see him as a Pied Piper: provided the image also conveys the essential fact that, in luring rats and children from their ordinary occupations, he also assumes responsibility for them.

But it is a responsibility different from that of the politician, the sociologist or the preacher. The writer remains a *writer*: the nature of his choice—to write rather than to go to Parliament or be a good Calvinist—implies a different relationship with the world.

We must face the simple fact that the actual effect of art as such is intimate and personal. The theatre critic Eric Bentley pointed out that Beethoven's Ninth Symphony has done less to create brotherhood among men than any performance by the Salvation Army. But he also insists that it would be ridiculous to reject Beethoven for that reason. What happens inside you when you see *Lear* or read *Crime and Punishment* or look at *Guernica* or listen to the *Well-tempered Clavichord* may be insignificant in comparison to the effects of a bomb, a speech by Mao Tse-Tung, a new law by Vorster or a riot in Harlem . . . but that it *has* an effect which, in its own right, can be tremendous, cannot be denied. And it should never be underestimated.

The work of art cannot—and need not—be justified on religious, political, moral or other grounds. But it satisfies a need in man which is as vital as hunger, even though it may not be recognized as readily. Like hunger, it is a personal need. But in its intimacy it is extremely significant. For it can expand an awareness of the human condition.

What the writer does essentially implies that his work, if it is worthwhile, acts as a conscience in the world.

IV

The operation of this conscience will, to a large extent, depend on the nature of the world within which it functions. Or, to be more precise, on what the writer perceives to be the nature of his world, since it is only from a profound involvement in the problems of his world that the writer turns to writing.

Now our world has been defined in innumerable ways, and these need not be mutually exclusive. But it seems to me that in *Art and Revolution* John Berger offered a diagnosis particularly relevant to the South Africa we live in today.

In Berger's view, shared by many others, most of the problems in the world today are related to the exploitation and degradation of people all over the world, and to their struggle to liberate themselves from the most humiliating of these forms of exploitation and degradation. This involves primarily the struggle in the Third World to become free from the imperialism of Europe, the United States and Russia—freedom, above all, from exploitation: economic, but also mental, moral, spiritual: freedom from the attitude that other people are there to be used, not as people, but as commodities. In the way Africans, coloureds and Indians have been reduced to commodities in our country.

Let us be quite clear about this aspect of the situation in our world: two-thirds of the people in the world are being exploited, deceived and humiliated by the remaining third. If this condition is accepted or, worse, institutionalized (as in South Africa), it can only be aggravated. For imperialism, whether economic or moral, is insatiable. We have reached a situation where no acceptance or justification of the status quo is permissible. Because the 'wretched of the earth', the dispossessed, the disinherited, have their identity taken from them. And once a man's identity is denied, a struggle is initiated which cannot end before he has found his place and his name again. This suffering is not reserved for the

47

already deprived: it exists in a peculiarly agonizing form in the minds of those who are *aware* of it: our torture, says Berger, is the existence of others as unequals. (Fanon: 'Leave this Europe where they are never done talking of Man, yet murder men everywhere they find them.')

One may ask: is there anything new in this condition? Has there not always been suffering and injustice and oppression? Of course. But until recently the condition of the world was not wholly intolerable—because the full measure of the truth was not known. Earlier, Europeans could deceive themselves, John Berger points out, by believing that they represented humanity at its most civilized: so they were not forced to abandon a final belief in equality, as the issue could be deferred while they exploited inequality. And the exploited natives of the world were not aware of the scale of what was perpetrated against them. Today South Americans, Asians and Africans have discovered the whole extent of what is taking place. And this creates despair. And fury. (Baldwin: 'We live in rage and pain, in rage and pain.') Mass communications have propagated these events around the world; and 'no man can claim that he has not personally SEEN the intolerable condition of the world'.

And the essence of this condition is, as Berger so eloquently points out, the fact that a minority of people are exploiting the markets and the minds of the rest, and regard them as expendable. Which means, he says, that each individual who fights imperialism in our world is also fighting for human meaning.

This, it seems to me, indicates a function of writers in our terrifying and sordid world: to keep the voice of humanity alive; to ensure the survival of human values.

Of course, 'human values,' like the 'human scope' I referred to earlier, is a notoriously vague term. Yet it is by no means impossible to attempt a clearer definition. For obvious reasons such a definition should start from a look at the individual human being, in order to find out which values in him can be so precious and at the same time so basic that the artist is willing to risk everything—time, the respect of others, peace of mind, love, even money—to fight for the preservation of their dignity.

We can start with the simplest characteristic of an individual: he is animate. Though most people seem more dead than alive, the biological fact is that man is alive and not dead.

And if this is the simplest characteristic of the human being—that he is alive—it is part of his dignity that he should have the right to live, and that no one should force him to die. But is this really as simple as it seems? Is it simple in a country where more crimes are punishable by death than in any other country in the world?

We must proceed. A person lives, we have decided. But what does that imply: *to live*? Again on the very basic level: it means to grow, to change, to move. On the other end of the scale lie decay and death.

And if the human condition begins with being alive, and if being alive demands that a person should move, should grow, and, in the process, change, then these will be human values worth rebelling for: then people should have the *right* to move, to grow and to change. And they should not be subjected unnecessarily to that which hampers growth, movement, change and which precipitates decay and death.

These attributes of life are not mere physical processes. They have metaphysical equivalents. For animals and plants, too, live. They, too, move and grow and change. But the human being is supposed to differ from them in his

49

possession of reason, in his awareness of—or quest for, or even uncertainty about—'something more'. People are the only creatures on earth not satisfied with being what they are. They want to be more, to become more, to become different.

Let us not argue about the soul. Let us accept what we more or less know and what we can more or less prove:

The human being has intelligence. In other words, he does not only experience, but he can interpret, associate, relate, anticipate experience. If he has this faculty, he also has the duty to use and develop it in the name of that movement, growth and change which we have identified on the biological level. And once again this implies that people should be respected in this dignity which lies in their *right* to think, to relate, to interpret. They should not be hampered in these processes: they should not be hindered in their task of relating today to yesterday and tomorrow.

Part of the means people have developed to express and embody these processes is to be found in language. People can speak, and read, and write: they should have a *right* to speak, to read, to write.

These activities all touch upon the individual's urge to communicate, which may be his most urgent physical and metaphysical need. And so he should have the right to communicate—or at least to *try* to communicate on all the levels of communication available to him, including the sexual, which is not only a biological function but the expression of a metaphysical enquiry. And so I should demand for him the right to choose his sexual partners and to interpret his sexual experience.

VI

But with communication we have crossed the border between the individual as a lonely being and that same individual as a social being. This is the consequence of human consciousness—and perhaps one of the noblest attributes which distinguish people from other animals: they can relate their experience to that of others. They can compare. What the individual demands, he demands not only for himself, but for others as well. Philogenesis is inextricably linked to ontogenesis. Here, too, we must accept that the metaphysical is rooted in the physical: for if a person lives, he has the urge to perpetuate his existence and to safeguard it.

In an absolutely personal sense this might lead to the negation or even annihilation of others. But because of the social dimension the individual's urge to protect himself implies that he should not harm others—since that might invite retaliation. Consequently I can only feel truly safe if I also protect the safety of others. Whatever one does through one's freedom of choice, should never unduly impair the freedom of others. Which means that freedom must be measured with justice.

In an absolute sense, as Camus insisted, these conditions are mutually exclusive: absolute freedom includes the freedom of the strong to suppress the weak; absolute justice curtails all separate liberties. Consequently they can only co-exist in a relative sense. They force one to accept that the human domain is the relative; which, by the same token, implies that one's freedom and one's justice can always be improved and enlarged. And it means that the writer should constantly rebel against the set of circumstances which imperil or curtail the freedom and justice of the individuals in *his* society and *his* world.

In the light of all this one can now return to the view of the writer as the rebel who fights in the name of the essentially human values—against everything which threatens the human, against everything which is essentially *inhuman*.

51

Let us not underestimate this task, and most especially not when it concerns the writer and his work in South Africa. For judging by its security legislation (aggravated by the recent introduction of a Bureau of State Security, so aptly abbreviated as BOSS), its pass laws and influx control laws, its Group Areas Act and its Immorality Act . . . this is not a 'human' country. The entire system which determines every aspect of private and communal life in the country is a contradiction of all the basic attributes we have termed 'human': movement; growth; change; communication; the right to think, to read, to speak, to write; the right to choose a sexual partner and relate one's experience to that of others; the right not to be killed; the small, precious, personal right to be—to be in awareness, in compassion, in humility, in defiance, in anger, in pain, and—if it must be so—in violence.

However, if I am pleading a literary cause, it is the cause of a literature wholly committed to humanity, which requires a peculiar *awareness* in those who write in this country. Awareness not of one's subjective problems only, and not only of the situation of the small *laager* of a few million whites . . . but awareness of the country as a whole and of its relation to the fierce world around us. Awareness, and courage, and humility. And a sense of loyalty to the truth, and to the imperative need to speak it fearlessly.

Will it have any 'effect'? I have pointed out how *in*effectual writing can be in practical terms. But also, I hope, of how wide its limits are. There are revolutions of many sorts in our world; Régis Debray, the young French revolutionary serving a thirty-year sentence in Bolivia, wrote 'Poor gun without a word, poor word without a gun.'

We are indeed living in the midst of a revolutionary situation which manifests itself in many ways and on many levels.

The revolution I am involved in as a writer, is a revolution in the conscience of my people. Perhaps it is not much I can accomplish—and I must demand of myself to be honest and to admit when an attitude becomes nothing more than rationalization. Indeed, it is a slow process. One can reach one person here, another there; after a long time we may still be only a handful. But I remember the words of Eluard:

They were but a handful—
Suddenly they were a crowd.

And it is in the light of this that I should like to repeat the dictum of Debray, but now reversed: 'Poor word without a gun: poor gun without a word.'

Mahatma Gandhi Today

(1970)

I feel very proud and very humble to have the privilege of delivering this Memorial Lecture just one year after the centenary of The Great Soul's birthday on 2 October 1869. It is now almost twenty-three years after that tragic day in January 1948 when the Mahatma was killed by the bullet of a fanatic, so soon after one of his noblest achievements through fasting: reconciling the two great rival religious groups in India. This was, as is so well known, one of the forms of expression of his justly famous peaceful weapon, *satyagraha*, 'Soul Force', which, many years before, he had also applied in South Africa to ease the oppression suffered by his compatriots in this country.

In recent years there have been many disturbing reports of new unrest and new strife, of the revival of old antagonisms in India. And as far as this country is concerned: the S. A. Indian Congress, founded by Gandhi and based on the very principle of *satyagraha*, has long been paralysed. What is more, those principles of love and co-operation of people of different races on a basis of equality, are insulted and denied daily by the unmitigated evil of the apartheid system which has got its deadly grip on our society like a boa constrictor on its prey. Millions of people are insulted and humiliated and oppressed and denied their simplest human dignity simply because their skin colour is less etiolated than that of an oppressor who has lived under a moral wheelbarrow for too long. And many thousands of people who sympathize with Gandhi's belief in a racial equality, in the common dignity of all men, are languishing in jail, in various forms of banishment, or in exile. In our beautiful and unhappy country a small minority is determining absolutely the lives of all and causing the deaths of many. And so it may seem as if the Mahatma is, in fact, dead; and as if his spirit of greatness and compassion has really departed from us.

But appearances are deceptive; and that is the theme of my lecture today. The Mahatma is dead. Yet the Mahatma will never be dead. And in mourning Mohandas Karamchand Gandhi today we also celebrate his undying legacy to the world.

I realized this very acutely in the past fortnight, à propos of another great man, in his way a disciple of Gandhi. In a letter in a Cape Town newspaper ex-judge Blackwell made an appeal for clemency for Bram Fischer who is at present, old and in poor health, serving a life sentence in jail. Given the authorities we have I doubt whether this plea will be heeded, although I most sincerely endorse it. But it was something else about the judge's newspaper letter which struck me even more. Bram Fischer, he said, was in danger of becoming a forgotten man. And in that, I think, he was wrong. I, for one, and there are many like me—and several Afrikaners among them—can never forget the impression made by Bram Fischer's profoundly moving statement from the dock before he was sentenced. It was, fortunately, widely reported at the time, and in the evolution of my own ethical and political thinking his statement marked a turning point, a decisive moment. I am not allowed to quote publicly from his speech, because even that is forbidden in this free country which the Prime Minister constantly assures us is not a police state. The important thing is that his ideals of racial harmony and co-operation did not go to jail with him. Nor did the memory of his compassion with those suffering on account of their race, his adherence to the principle that everybody should be allowed to help determine the form of government which shapes his life.

The government—*any* government—can effectively silence or incapacitate an individual or even large numbers of individuals, but all the battalions of fear and all the organizations of hate, all the formidable, destructive power of armies and police, of Saracens and jails, of BOSS-laws and banishments cannot kill an idea in which the light of truth is burning.

And it occurred to me, as I read Judge Blackwell's letter, that even when Fischer dies those words he spoke in the dock would live by virtue of the simple fact that I, and many others, can never forget them. And when we, too, die one day, a new generation will be at hand to keep those ideals alive. I am reminded of an essay by the great Afrikaans poet Van Wyk Louw, 'Heerser en Humanis' ('Tyrant and Humanist'), in which, on the eve of his execution, a condemned writer is visited in jail by the head of state. The tyrant promises him a reprieve on the condition that he recant. If not, he will die and every word he has ever written will be destroyed. With quiet assurance the humanist elects to die, bolstered by the conviction that he will win in the end. 'How can that be?' the tyrant asks. 'I have two reasons,' replies the condemned man. 'One is that your executioner will see me die. The other is that you have found it necessary to visit me tonight.'

It may be helpful to dwell a bit more on the history of Bram Fischer, for the sake of those who have already begun to forget about him; and also for his illumination of the spirit of Gandhi.

The many who have come to think of Fischer as a bogeyman, as a symbol of darkness and evil which threaten to destroy South Africa, should be reminded that he belongs to one of the most prominent families of Orange Free State history. His father, a respected lawyer, was a mediator between the Transvaal and Britain before the Anglo-Boer War and later became Prime Minister of the Orange River Colony. He played a leading role in the drafting of the constitution of the Union of South Africa. His son became one of the most brilliant advocates in South African legal history.

Yet this remarkable man grew up as an ordinary Afrikaans farm boy. At an early age he embraced the doctrine of racial segregation as a solution for the problems of his country; and at one stage, in his own admission, he found it almost impossible to shake hands with a black man.

It was only during a period of soul-searching and mental agony that he discovered, in Hitler's terrible ascent, what the logical outcome of a theory of racial superiority was. Still he found it difficult to shed his convictions. One night, in a discussion with an elderly African, he put forward the hackneyed theory that segregation diminishes points of friction. The old man countered by pointing out that if one separates the races into different camps, the inhabitants of either camp soon forget that the others laugh and suffer and live in the same way and for the same reasons; and so they soon become suspicious—until they learn to fear one another, which is where all racism starts.

From these elementary beginnings Fischer's uncompromising intellect soon set him on the way towards Marxism. However, it was not primarily the theory of Marxism which attracted him, but, quite simply, the practical realities of the land he lived in. These realities were twofold: in the first place, there was the pattern of oppression which characterizes and dominates South African society. What would happen, he wondered, if, suddenly, all Afrikaners were herded into the Orange Free State as their 'homeland' and forced to carry passes when they left it; if all the gold and coal mines of the Free State were kept in black hands, and if Afrikaners working elsewhere in the country were forced to live in locations and compounds, allowed to do unskilled work only, and if their very presence outside the Free State were only on sufferance of another race . . . ? In the second place he discovered that the only people prepared to suffer for convictions similar to his—people who could have all the luxury they wanted if they chose, but who identified themselves to such an extent with the deprived majority that they were prepared to forgo all that and risk imprisonment, banishment, or even death—were members of the Communist Party. At that time, of course, the Party was completely legal on the SA political scene, so that for a law-abiding legal man like Fischer it was the natural platform for his convictions.

When the Party was outlawed in the 1950s, Fischer realized that the measure had very little to do with anti-communism as such, but that it was essentially a measure to silence opposition to the accelerating process of safeguarding white interests at the cost of black liberties. And so, with much agonizing soul-searching, Fischer remained a member·of the banned Party, with only one firm intention, that of helping to create a truly democratic society in the country, in which white and black would be able to decide together on their communal future.

Fischer often expressed his belief in the inevitability of the historical process: in these terms history is not an accumulation of chaotic facts and figures, but a logical development from one form of society to another. At an early stage he became convinced that the only true form compatible with the demands of the present century was Socialism. But he also believed that South Africa was not ready for it, and so he refused to impose it on the country. He knew that we had reached a stage of breakdown in the history of capitalism and imperialism, since these two great forces, which had dominated the nineteenth century, were unable to fulfil the needs of twentieth-century people. At the same time he saw that, at the very moment when imperialism was breaking down all over Africa, leading to the emergence of new states and systems, a small and desperate band of whites were trying to preserve it in South Africa, leading to more and more suffering, and to more and more oppression.

During all his free life Fischer wanted to work for the restoration of human dignity. And he accepted that it could be done only through non-violent measures. Time and time again he insisted that bloodshed would create intolerable chaos. At the same time he saw that South Africa was moving constantly closer to a state of terrorism and civil war: and, drawing on the experience of Algeria (with today's perspective he might have added Vietnam) he realized that in such a war there could be only one outcome. This prospect was against his belief, which was also Nelson Mandela's, in the creation of a just and tolerant multi-racial society with white and black working together for the future of the country they all shared.

And it was to warn South Africa against the destructive end of its own present course that he finally went beyond Gandhi's strategies and embarked, with others, on a programme of controlled sabotage. Controlled, because every target was selected so carefully that there would never be any possibility of danger to life or limb. It was done as an act of despair, to warn the authorities against their own folly, and to help create a climate in which the need for togetherness would supersede the urge towards separateness which was tearing his country apart.

One may quarrel with his means, but not with his aims. Today, after the crisis in Mozambique, more and more white South Africans are beginning to see the wisdom of moving towards a realization of Fischer's ideals. Only, he saw it much sooner, and much more clearly and without self-interest or personal ambition.

Knowing that he was risking his life, he came back to South Africa in 1964 after being allowed to go to England to plead a case before the Privy Council. He could have stayed out, a free man. Yet he came back to certain imprisonment and a possible death sentence. When he estreated bail after being arrested, it was not to save his skin, but for the sake of continuing to work for the cause he believed in—the cause for which so many of his friends were by then languishing in jail. He knew that many of those victims had placed all responsibility for their condition on the shoulders of the Afrikaner rulers. And so he wanted to prove that an Afrikaner could also be different.

His free life was devoted to a broadening of the image of the Afrikaner; and if Afrikaans is eventually to survive as a language, much of it will be due to the fact that men like Bram Fischer have been prepared to prove, risking their all for it, that it is more than the language of one oppressive minority and of one frightening ideology—that it is indeed what many exiles call it today: *menstaal*, 'the language of human beings'.

That is why I feel so confident that Fischer can never be forgotten in this country. And I referred to him at some length because in his awareness of and concern for others, in his compassion, in his crusade against social and political evil, he revealed himself as a man true to the spirit of the Great Soul we mourn and celebrate today: Mohandas Karamchand Gandhi.

A mere three weeks before his death, as he commenced his final fast, Gandhi proclaimed his willingness to die in the process: 'No man, if he is pure, has anything more precious to give than his life. I hope and pray that I have that purity in me to justify the step'—this was an act, above all a readiness, an inner preparedness, comparable to the immolation of Buddhist monks protesting against the senseless violence of American aggression in Vietnam or the self-sacrifice of a young Czech student to protest against the Russian occupation of his country in 1968. More than anything else the Mahatma reminds me of the words of Christ: 'There is no greater love than this, that a man should lay down his life for his friends.' And I make this link deliberately, because Gandhi himself often acknowledged that the first great influence on the evolution of his own credo was the Sermon on the Mount: that immortal expression of the power of meekness, the force of humility, the inevitable victory of compassion. Gandhi knew that meekness was not weakness. And by making the supreme sacrifice, he also proved that he knew what protest really meant.

It was Jean-Paul Sartre who drew the most relevant distinction I know between a gesture and an act. A gesture, he said, is something performed by an actor, intended for an audience: we can evaluate the gesture as good or bad, as successful or unsuccessful, but it really exists in a void: it has no practical or even moral significance. A gesture takes place without reference to cause and effect, without consequence. An act, on the other hand, in Sartre's definition, implies involvement in the whole chain of cause and effect: it leads to something, it has a direct moral or practical bearing on the situation in which it is performed; and thereby it *commits* the man who performs it. It is in this commitment that the basic difference between a Sartrean gesture and an act is to be found. We are living in a world where various forms of protest, violent and non-violent, have become almost a way of living. But so much of it—in this country too— is mere gesture, without full commitment. Gandhi knew the deepest implications of commitment; because it is only in the willingness to sacrifice that commitment is tested. That is the difference between the demo and the true rebel—in the sense in which Buddha and Christ and Mohammed and Gandhi and Paul Kruger and Bram Fischer were rebels.

I believe in rebellion as a dimension of existence; in fact, as a prerequisite for life. Not blind rebellion. But rebellion in the sense of breaking constantly more fetters limiting true human liberty. The slave who rebels against his master, said Camus, does not do so merely to be free: he does it in order to affirm the necessity of freedom as the human condition.

In other words, it is a rebellion not simply directed *against* something, but aimed towards something. It is not negative, but positive. When Antigone—the first rebel of Western tradition—revolted against the State, it was not because she wanted to destroy order, but because she wanted to affirm a higher Order than that maintained by the State. Antigone's key word is: NO! But it is a paradoxical thing, for she really means: YES. *No* to all the forces which try to deny the human; *yes* to all the attributes of dignified human life. Gandhi added a specific religious dimension when he said: 'I know that I shall never know God if I do not wrestle with and against evil, even at the cost of life itself.'

This essentially human, metaphysical revolt—which works through on all levels of one's existence—takes place in a world where there is, of necessity, a conflict between freedom and justice. Gandhi realized this implicitly as Camus did explicitly. In absolute form, justice and freedom are mutually exclusive: absolute freedom gives me the freedom also to limit another man's freedom, even to deny him life, to kill him; absolute justice denies the merits of the individual situation and works only with common denominators. Absolute freedom makes the individual all-powerful; absolute justice makes society an absolute power. So we can never have absolute freedom—but we can always have *more* freedom; and we can never have absolute justice—but we can always have *more* justice. In the balance between these two forces the individual and society meet each other. And this is precisely the territory on which Gandhi conducted his campaign of love, his war of peace.

It is this campaign which we can reassess today in the light of the conditions and needs prevalent in present-day South Africa. It is a campaign based on a series of clearly formulated precepts, all of them pervaded by the intense religiousness of Gandhi's philosophy and the humility and basic humanity of his personality.

1. Gandhi's vow of *swadeshi* seems strange to many people, particularly to Westerners. He himself defined it as 'that spirit within us which restricts us to the use and service of our immediate surroundings to the exclusion of the more remote'. To him it had a definite religious, political and economic significance, related to the very old concept of patriotism, of loyalty to one's own. In this respect one is reminded, again, of Van Wyk Louw's concept of 'loyal resistance'.

In the hands and minds of lesser men this notion of loyalty can very easily become a mere instrument of chauvinism; in the hands of the political leaders of this country today it is used as a slogan to keep people together in a small and stifling *laager* dominated by worn-out traditions: it is a negative approach, using fear to prevent people from dissenting, even from questioning, and it uses censorship and indoctrination to condition the writing, the reading and eventually the thinking of an entire generation.

To act against this, I should suggest a wider interpretation of *swadeshi* for this country at this time: I should suggest that we see it as loyalty, not to a party, or a church, or an economic system, or a language group, or a race, but loyalty to South Africa, to this country which is much more than the sum of her people, and much more permanent than any regime. I should like to see it as an unflinching and uncompromising demand for only the best and highest of human values for this country: which means an equally uncompromising resistance to everything which degrades humanity and denies dignity, everything which favours small in-groups, everything which is secondhand and inferior, and shopsoiled by irreverent politicians. Above all, let our form of *swadeshi* be a demand for truth and justice in this country. There is very little truth and very little justice in

63

the world. But lies and injustice in any corner of this world should never allow us to condone it here. In this way *swadeshi* becomes a force to destroy evil and hypocrisy and inhumanity and to preserve the most sacred values of a multi-racial society intact. It implies Gandhi's direct statement that 'politics, divorced from religion, has absolutely no meaning.' And it denies the form of politics perpetrated in this country today, where religion is used as a serf of politics and a pretext for the most blatant exploitation of the majority of South Africans by a minority. 'Indian nationalism,' said Gandhi, 'is not exclusive, nor aggressive, nor destructive.' What we have in South Africa today, is a Nationalism which *is* exclusive, aggressive and destructive, and which inevitably evokes forms of resistance that may become equally exclusive, aggressive and destructive. It should be part of our interpretation of *swadeshi* to substitute the original for the vicious fake, and not to rest before the fake has been eliminated—in the name of the real South Africa.

2. Gandhi's ethics of *khaddar* ('Homespun cloth', i.e. work in the widest sense of the word) is closely linked with *swadeshi*. To him it meant a specific form of home-industry to counter the exploitation inherent in the more imperialistic forms of capitalism. Today industrialization is an irreversible fact. But in our context *khaddar* may certainly be interpreted to mean the intimate relation between a man and his work: the demand that a man should bear responsibility for his work in order to lend it dignity; and that he should share in the fruits of his labour. In other words: no man should be exploited in his work or alienated through his work. The whole of the South African economy is based on the exploitation of men, women and children with a black skin, and the policy of 'homelands' is an impossible and inhuman dream. It accepts that people can be used for the labour they can provide, without acknowledging even in the most basic sense of the word, that they are *people*.

64

Insisting on the essential dignity of work means revolting against the entire system which promotes economic and spiritual exploitation of one man by another. 'The supreme consideration,' says Gandhi, 'is man.'

3. This concept is intimately associated with Gandhi's religious background as a conservative Hindu, living within the framework of a Hindu caste society. He accepts the inevitability, in many ways even the necessity of caste, but— in his own words—'not to restrict or regulate social intercourse'. For his views on caste are based on his fundamental assumption that, even as a devout Hindu, he cannot accept Hinduism as an exclusive religion. In other words: accepting, as premise, the existence of different religions and different castes, he nevertheless accepted them in a completely 'open' sense: 'Let us not deny God,' he writes in one essay, 'by denying to a fifth of our race the right of association on an equal footing.' Transposed into South African terms it would read: 'Let us not deny to 80 per cent of our people the right of association on an equal footing.'

Given the existence of different groups, Gandhi insists that all men and women are essentially brothers and sisters. Some pious advocates of apartheid proclaim—and some of them actually believe—that this system eliminates the possibility of friction and creates an atmosphere for happier and more complete self-realization. But this denies the essential fact that separation and the barriers it constructs between people can only lead to suspicion and fear and hate. In a world already overpopulated, in which mass media and international communication systems are rapidly eliminating all artificial barriers and increasing contact, South Africa alone tries to reverse the process by erecting more and more barriers between people—aimed at the final utopia of apartheid, with separate heavens, separate hells, and separate lavatories for all.

Without denying one iota of the inherent differences distinguishing individuals and groups, we have a need today, more urgent than ever before, of Gandhi's vision of the common dignity of all men. 'The only thing that is really worth while,' said one writer, 'is being together.' He said it of man and woman, of lovers. We should say it, as Gandhi did, of people—of all the people in this country. All it requires is the acknowledgement of the *fact* that we are all here together, sharing this country, and that we are all equal in our love of it.

4. And now we come to what, for a Westerner, is an extremely difficult aspect of Gandhi's credo as a Hindu: that is, his tenacious belief in the Hindu custom of Cow Protection as a religious obligation. To many this may seem parochial or outdated. To the Mahatma it was an essential part of his philosophy. But the important thing is that he also said: 'I believe in Cow Protection in a much larger sense than the popular belief.' As I interpret it, it is not so much the cow *as cow* that matters to him—for then cow-worship can easily degenerate into a fossilized symbol which can prevent the true and full development of a community. It is rather that he saw the cow as—in his own magnificent phrase—'a poem of pity'. The cow, cherished beyond all treasures in early Hindu society, is gentleness and plenty incarnate. The life of the community depends on her milk: she should be protected and loved. And she is never aggressive: she bears patiently whatever misfortunes befall her—and that is why she eventually survives. In this I find, for our situation, the humble but necessary demand for a *reverence for life*.

We live in what is essentially a violent society. Alcohol—suicide—murder—assault—insanity—road accidents—all of these are symptoms of our violent society. Even South Africa's national sport, rugby, is popular because of its violence. I should not like to sound pedantic: but could not one reason for the incredible proliferation of violence in South Africa be a basic disrespect for life, a disrespect for others? And why? Once again I find the roots in apartheid. A system which uproots whole communities, which callously shrugs at deaths in prisons and prison vans, which forbids families to live together, and which is based on discriminating laws and humiliating measures like reference books, 'immorality', which restricts a man's advancement in his work and limits his income, which forces the majority of citizens to use third- and fourth-rate beaches and places of entertainment and which prohibits their attending theatre performances or symphony concerts . . . such a system has as its premise the conviction that man's life is not worth two sparrows. It turns man into an object, and once he is dehumanized, anything can be done to him without any qualms. Gandhi revered cows. We do not even revere people. It is time for such a system to be eradicated in order to create a new scope of life for people; in order to create a society in which human beings can be acknowledged simply for what they are: human beings.

5. And with this we have reached the two final, and basic, forces in Gandhi's life and work: the *vow of truth*, and the *vow of non-violence*.

Gandhi's injunction to be faithful to truth contains the intrinsic and explicit demand that one shall never be afraid of speaking the truth or of bringing it to light. 'I found through my wanderings in India', he said, 'that my country is seized with a paralysing fear. We may not open our lips in public: we may only talk about our opinions secretly . . . I suggest to you that there is only one whom we have to fear, that is God. When we fear God, then we shall fear no man, however high-placed he may be; and if you want to follow the vow of truth, then fearlessness is absolutely necessary.'

His description of India as a State of Fear strikes one as singularly familiar. Ours is indeed a Society of Fear. The authorities use fear to strengthen their hold on the people. Individuals fear lest by speaking the truth they will be prosecuted. Let us shake off the bond of fear and proclaim the truth wherever we find it, and however dangerous it appears. Truth is always dangerous: that is why authorities prefer to keep it hidden from view. And one basic truth hidden very securely in South Africa is the fact that society is not a fate which must be endured as if it had been handed down by God: it is a practical organization of men, by men, for men—and it can and must be changed when it no longer expresses adequately the wishes and needs of the individuals within it.

After twenty-two years of Nationalist domination a whole generation of people in South Africa know no other rule and seem to resign themselves to its inevitability. But it need *not* be suffered as a fate. It can be changed. It must be changed, for it has long ceased to be—it never was—the expression of the needs and wishes of the majority of people in the country. There is one force that can kill the fear which often threatens to paralyse us when we wish to bring the truth to light. That force is the love which 'drives out fear'.

For love is in the centre of Gandhi's teaching of *ahimsa* which is, in Milton's words, 'the irresistible might of meekness'. Literally *ahimsa* means 'non-killing'. Hence its usual translation as 'non-violence' or 'passive resistance', both of which terms were severely disliked by Gandhi. For it is not a negative but a positive force. And the power within it is love: 'To one who follows this doctrine there is no room for an enemy . . . But I go further. If we resent a friend's action, or a so-called enemy's action, we still fall short of this doctrine.'

Then follows the very important qualification: 'When I say we should not resent, I do not say that we should acquiesce.' In fact, Gandhi states that it means the opposite of acquiescence: he illustrates how a surgeon can wield his knife on the patient's body for the latter's benefit, cutting out disease in order to heal, practising, in the process, 'the purest Ahimsa'. Likewise, *ahimsa* demands of us to rebel actively against all evil and not to rest before it has been destroyed: 'Ahimsa is a positive state of love, of doing good even to the evil-doer. It does not mean helping the evil-doer to continue the wrong or tolerating it by passive acquiescence. On the contrary, love requires you to resist the wrong-doer by dissociating yourself from him even though it may offend him or injure him physically.'

This is the supreme message of Gandhi, as exemplified by his whole life and very specifically by his *satyagraha* in South Africa: there was nothing 'passive' about his resistance—and certainly no consideration for personal comfort or safety. His imprisonment and constant persecution prove this very eloquently. He practised, as fully as he preached, this form of resistance, insisting that 'Soul-Force is infinitely superior to body-force. If people, in order to secure redress of wrongs, resorted to Soul-Force, much of the present suffering would be avoided. There is no such thing as failure in the use of this kind of force. "Resist not evil" means that evil is not to be repelled by evil but by good.'

Something achieved through violence, Gandhi rightly maintains, can be held only through violence. Something achieved through the highest activity of a mind bent on love and on doing good, on opposing evil by good, can be retained simply by remaining worthy of it.

It can be argued that Gandhi's adversaries, the British, with at least a token tradition of 'doing the gentlemanly thing' might have been more susceptible to moral persuasion than the South African Government would be in similar circumstances; that Gandhi's *satyagraha* would have availed nothing against Hitler. It may also be argued that some situations become so inextricably bound up with violence that only violence can break the deadlock. What Gandhi indicated was that violence, in its gross oversimplifications, is always an insult to humanity—to the man who has recourse to it as much as to the victim. And what he does make eminently clear is that, whatever road South Africa may choose in the future, whether that of violent revolution or of relatively peaceful change, there can be no victory over evil unless there is Soul-Force in the struggle, unless those of us committed to the fight against oppression and injustice are also *morally* superior to our adversaries.

If we evaluate, in the light of everything Gandhi represented, the situation in South Africa today and agree on the need for urgent and radical change, we should be reminded by his example that change involves more than the destruction of what exists, more than the replacement of one system by another: it is a process directed inward as much as outward, to the self as much as to the other. It involves, in the words of a poem dear to the Mahatma, a movement from the unreal to the Real, from darkness to Light, from death to Deathlessness. What we need is to change the country into a better place to live in, and ourselves into people more worthy of living in it.

On Culture and Apartheid

(1970)

The object of this paper is to examine some aspects of the cultural situation in South African apartheid society, notably the social implications of some specific cultural phenomena; and to attempt an evaluation of some possibilities of social change in the light of cultural development. My contribution is intended as no more than a brief introduction to the subject, and although I shall aim at objectivity it must be made very clear at the outset that the nature of my examination is personal.

This means that the terms of my approach must be defined.

1. Although this paper forms part of a specifically *Christian* project, I must insist that I am not a Christian and cannot, therefore, approach the subject as a Christian. I do, however, subscribe to the basic Christian values: to justice; to compassion which transcends justice; to individual liberty which respects the liberty of others; to a concept of human dignity which accepts that all men are equal; above all, to *caritas* in its widest sense.

2. I am a writer, not a politician. And so I may not always be practical in my approach. I most emphatically deny, however, that ethical ideals should be regarded as unpractical or impracticable simply because they are ideals.

Convictions, if strong enough, can turn almost any ideal into a practical possibility.

3. I believe in the metaphysical concept of revolt as defined by Camus. I believe that apartheid is a denial of everything that is basic to human dignity and to the concept of love; therefore I am dedicated to the ideal of changing it. Peacefully, if possible, because it seems to me that violence denies not only the humanity of the person against which it is directed but also that of the person who practises it. At the same time I acknowledge, with Camus, that there may be some situations in which violence appears to many to be the only option: and it seems to me that South Africa is fast approaching that point of no return where violence may be unavoidable. At the same time I am convinced that at this stage there is still a possibility of effecting change peacefully. But this means *change*, not *compromise*. Compromise, adaptation, token resistance can all be 'contained' by the system and, in fact, imply condonation of system. And if a system is as odious and inhuman as apartheid any condonation of it violates one's own integrity.

4. Ideally, the concept of 'culture' should be more precisely defined in advance, but that would demand a paper in its own right. (In 1968 an entire UNESCO conference was devoted to an exploration of this concept without arriving at any clear conclusion.) If one accepts culture as the sum total of everything that is 'acquired' by man, in the process of civilization, to define and organize and shape his position and his behaviour and his attitudes in society—then it should be clear how wide this concept really is. For the purposes of this paper we may limit ourselves to some accepted manifestations of culture: arts and crafts; language; recreation and entertainment; sport, etc. (Obviously religion also forms part of it, and a nation's whole 'way of life' is embodied in it—the way it organizes its politics and its justice and its education and its urban development programmes—but these aspects are treated by other *Spro-cas* commissions

and so fall beyond the immediate scope of this paper.) In the present context it is of some relevance to approach culture as the body of habits, conventions and behaviour patterns which allows an individual to express himself in a social context and to be comprehended: i.e., that body of patterns or structures which most clearly distinguishes one society, one nation, sometimes one race, from another without denying their underlying 'human universality'.

I

The first fact one has to bear in mind is that there is no single 'South African culture': this is a multi-cultural society. Ever since Stockenström's Kat River Settlement and Sir Benjamin D'Urban's administration of the first 'Bantu Homeland' (the Province of Queen Adelaide) in the first half of the nineteenth century, the concept of separate groups and separate group cultures has become entrenched as 'the South African way of life'. This system, imposed largely by British colonialists, has contributed to the isolation of different local cultures. On the other hand, there have been strong forces at work *against* cultural isolation: political unification in 1910, the complex economic interdependence of the different groups, the comparative accessibility of two official languages, urbanization, the rapid development of national and international communications, the impact of the mass media, etc. In other words: in spite of the existence of a variety of cultures in South Africa, by *c.* 1948 there was evidence of a tendency towards assimilation, a gradual development in the direction of a new holistic cultural structure. (In at least one field this had become manifest by 1948: the cultural unity of Afrikaners and coloureds.)

The introduction of apartheid as a political structure made an end to amalgamation as a 'natural impulse' (in the words of Lewis Nkosi). Culturally, the premise of apartheid was that

73

separate development would provide equal facilities for all groups. With the preservation of their 'own identities' all groups would then fully develop their cultural potential and, in the words of the old dictum, be true to their own selves. So lofty was this ideal that Dr Verwoerd could state, without batting an eyelid, 'We shall be able to prove that it is only by creating separate nations that discrimination will in fact disappear in the long run' (4 December 1963: note, incidentally, the significance of the word 'creating'!). Since 1948 this separation has grown more and more dogmatic and rigid: separate sports, separate concerts, separate beaches, separate libraries, separate churches, separate educational systems (with mother tongue instruction for all African sections), separate radio programmes, separate universities.

If this incredible structure of separation had in fact stimulated growth of all—or even some—different cultures in the country, it would have been difficult wholly to discredit it. But the reverse is all too sadly true.

In the first place, amenities and facilities made available to the different groups have *not* been similar. However outdated or hypocritical, the nineteenth-century American slogan of 'separate but equal' might still have had some virtue if the requirement of equality had in fact been respected. But this did not happen. It is not necessary to accumulate statistics. One look at the allocation of beaches to the different race groups is enough to expose the farce of 'equal cultural opportunities'. Another look at libraries confirms it. (In 1964 the Pietermaritzburg White Library contained 4,890 reference books; the African branch of the library had 2 volumes.) The almost insuperable difficulties encountered by regional Councils for the Performing Arts to present occasional performances to non-white audiences speak for themselves. Academic standards in the African and coloured universities are appalling. The state of African education is a disgrace for any responsible government (the State spends *ten times* as much on the education of a white child as on that of a black). Sports facilities for blacks are ludicrously inadequate . . .

In other words: cultural separation has meant *cultural deprivation* to almost all non-white groups. Black school children cannot attend performances of prescribed plays if these are produced by whites; it is almost impossible for a black to attend a symphony concert or even a folk music performance by an imported pop singer. Barely 10 per cent of all films on circuit in the country are shown to non-white audiences. Consequently, these group cultures, representing the overwhelming majority of the South African population, yet deprived of almost all stimulation from outside, are forced to exploit only the material immediately available within each group—and even for that there are hardly any facilities or funds. This means that 'culture' has become a privilege for a small minority. Whereas essentially culture is not a privilege but an elementary human right, an indispensable human dimension. In a scathing and justified attack on South African culture Breyten Breytenbach blamed the 'tribal whites' of the country for 'reducing culture to folklore'. The white concept of African culture, he says, is limited to Ndebele huts, Xhosa pots or Zulu beads. Coloured 'culture', to whites, means the Cape Coon Carnival of 2 January—and even that has been rigidly regimented: the only authentic, spontaneous indigenous folk festival in the country has become subjected to tight control in order not to inconvenience the privileged whites through whose area the dancers traditionally held their gay procession.

It would be wrong, however, to think—be it sadly or smugly—that only non-whites have suffered from cultural malnutrition: white culture, both English and Afrikaans, has been affected as deeply, if more subtly. Quite recently Guy Butler still had to admit that most English South African poets still regarded London or New York as their spiritual home: I do not think this is due to any atavistic colonial sentiment but to the fact that indigenous South African

75

cultures (African, coloured or Indian) have become more and more inaccessible to English speakers. This is certainly true of many Afrikaans writers.

One of the fiercest accusations history may make against apartheid will be that the Afrikaans writer has been cut off from Africa. When, in the magazine *Kol*, Breyten Breytenbach asked—in 1968—why Afrikaans writers never bother to visit African writers, an Afrikaans author replied: 'What African writer has ever looked *me* up?' One may dismiss this as a mere symptom of suprematism; but one should link it to another statement by the same author recently in the London *Times*. We Afrikaans writers, he said, yearn for Africa and need her . . . but Africa doesn't seem to need us. Once again one cannot hide one's dismay: after all, why the hell should Africa regard the writings of the Sestigers as significant or relevant in any way? But again this reveals the pathos—if not the tragedy—of cultural apartheid. At a moment when most of humanity is deeply conscious of Africa, at a moment when youth all over the world is discovering Africa, *we who live here* are denied ready access to the continent we live in, the continent that has shaped us. It is impossible to visit most African countries—because of apartheid. It is almost impossible to associate with African writers—because apartheid has either driven those writers out of the country, or imprisoned them, or made them almost impossible to reach (in every sense of the word). Where apartheid does not make it physically impossible to associate, it creates barriers of mistrust, suspicion or downright antagonism—*among people who would normally be drawn to one another* by their mutual interests.

In this situation the (younger) Afrikaans writer finds himself in a peculiar position. Almost all writers of the younger generation suffer from cultural schizophrenia. Because most of them have lived in Europe for longer or shorter periods, and because of the writer's natural inclination towards the larger philosophies and ideas of his time, they write their books from a world whose common denominators have been created by Sartre and Camus, by Henry Miller and Ionesco and Beckett: an international and cosmopolitan world. On the other hand, their very language ties them to a specific cultural group—a group which, through apartheid, through geographical necessity, and through the rigidities of Calvinism, has made a virtue of isolationism; a group almost wholly out of touch with the 'world outside'. And it becomes increasingly difficult to solve this duality. Especially because the majority of younger writers feel a very strong emotional and spiritual bond with 'our people' and prefer to adopt a defensive attitude towards the hostile outside world. This means that, contrary to trends almost everywhere else, young Afrikaans writers openly or tacitly support the Establishment; and this leads to the extreme of explicitly or implicitly endorsing, condoning, supporting Afrikaner Nationalism—and apartheid. The fear of rejection is incredibly strong in Afrikaans society— because that society has habitually been isolated (also geographically) from the rest of the world. To be ostracized from this community means to be literally 'thrown into the wilderness'. Because of the writer's association with Europe and America he may not feel quite so impotent as some of his predecessors—hence a reasonable measure of revolt in Afrikaans writing recently. It certainly is significant that the only recent cultural development within the apartheid system has been one based on revolt. But it has been, by and large, a relatively safe revolt: it knows how far it can go in confronting religious and moral taboos without rocking the political boat. Consequently even this tentative 'literature of revolt' has so far been largely contained by the system.

On the other hand, much recent writing by black South Africans has been marred by a narrow bitterness—most understandably so, for they have often suffered personal persecution; and most of them have had their books banned. Almost all the leading African and coloured writers of the country are now forced to live in exile. (And who cares about them? Nat Nakasa wrote the horrible truth: 'Most white South Africans have simply never opened their eyes to the reality of there being other humans beside the whites in this country. They do not "do unto others", but unto an unidentified mass of Natives.') How can they possibly avoid getting bogged down in personal resentment? Yet the loss of creativity, the loss of larger *dimensions* in much of this writing—directly attributable to apartheid—is one of the main arguments against the deliberate separation of cultures which leads, not to development, but to stagnation. The narrowness in white literature is equally evident. In most Afrikaans writing there is an irksome awareness of 'them' and 'us', a denial of the humanity of the Other; in much English writing the 'cause' is so important as to obscure an identification with living individuals.

Censorship has aggravated the situation. In spite of massive resistance from (white) artists and writers the Publications and Entertainments Act came into force in 1963. This Act, ostensibly directed primarily against attacks on religious or moral values, is essentially a political instrument. The Government realized, as many writers at the time did not, that religious and sexual emancipation indeed has political consequences: and so, to safeguard a 'traditional way of life' these newly won freedoms had to be curtailed in time. In this respect the South African Censorship Act is directly opposed to modern trends of liberalization all over the free world.

It soon became abundantly clear how effectively the Act could be used. Apart from keeping thousands of books out of the country (including works by some of the world's greatest writers and philosophers) and banning almost 90 per cent of all important overseas films, the Act has made it possible to ban the work of almost all the leading South African writers from the African and coloured groups, as well as that of several English South African writers, including Nadine Gordimer and Jack Cope.

Until now, no work by an Afrikaans author has been banned. It may be—as has been facetiously suggested—that no Afrikaans work has yet merited banning. But this may be due to other reasons too (because in several instances there have been very strong pressures from influential sections of Afrikanerdom to obtain bannings). These may include that mystical but extremely important sense of 'Afrikaner unity': if an individual Afrikaner is reluctant to find himself driven into the wilderness, the Afrikaner establishment is itself reluctant to drive a 'member of the family' out unless it becomes utterly unavoidable. Again this probably has historical and geographical roots: one should not weaken the *laager* in the wilderness. And so, if the Afrikaans writer has been allowed more scope than his English-speaking, coloured, Indian or African compatriots, it may be because the establishment is afraid of open rifts and prefers—for the time being—to suffer more from its own children than commit the terrible act of ostracism. Unfortunately, it would appear that Afrikaans writers have not made sufficient use of this scope allowed them. They have had this comparative liberty: why have they not exploited it?

Of course, censorship does not always work openly or legally. The climate of fear and suspicion created by the existence of a Censorship Act is often much more inhibiting than any action in terms of the law itself. It is obviously impossible to know whether any works of merit have remained unwritten as a result of fear of censorship—although we have the word of Etienne Leroux and others that some novels they would have liked to write have not been written. What can be asserted, however, is that the climate surrounding the Censorship Act has caused several works to remain unpublished. In 1964 at least four Sestiger writers were planning books dealing with sabotage, detention without trial, and similar subjects. Of these at least two were completed, Jan Rabie's *Die Agitator* and my *Die Saboteurs*. I do not know the full history of Rabie's novel. I know, however, that mine was accepted for publication on literary grounds—and then returned after consultation with lawyers. And I know that Breytenbach's novel *Om te Vlieg* was accepted on two occasions (on the recommendation of at least two professors of literature) and then returned—once because political pressure was exerted on the directors of the publishing house, and the second time because printers refused to take the risk of printing the book, for fear of prosecution. Even from Breytenbach's latest volume of poetry *Kouevuur (Cold Fire)* several of the best poems had to be omitted because printers feared prosecution—and also because they feared discrimination by other influential and wealthy clients. One firm has refused to print certain books because they might lose the patronage of the Dutch Reformed Church; another has been intimidated by the Salvation Army. I can cite several other instances, but these should prove the point.

The advocates of apartheid insist that the hardships and injustices (cultural and other) created by the system are temporary and belong by their very nature to a period of transition: these are, of course, the same arguments that have been advanced for decades by leaders in Russia, Hungary, China or East Germany. Furthermore: if non-whites in South Africa are to remain culturally deprived until they have fully developed their own states—how in God's name can they start from scratch then? Artificially to 'create' a culture is as impossible as Verwoerd's dream of 'creating' nations. In the meantime, the hard reality of our cultural situation is: for the whites, a narrowing of the world, inbreeding or escapism; for others, restriction, prosecution and denial.

Perhaps it should be stressed, again, that our form of censorship is a terrifyingly logical consequence of the apartheid mentality: it is based on the assumption that a handful of people have the—God-given?—*right* to decide what all the others may do, or read, or write, or think, or be. Which exposes this attitude as not merely inhuman but antihuman. Would it really be so preposterous to ascribe, at least in part, even our high fatality rate on the roads to the apartheid mentality which must deny the humanity of another person in order to survive oneself: once another person's humanity is denied, he can be destroyed, because he is no longer a *person*. In this connection the apartheid society—especially in its cultural implications—becomes a startling proof of the existential schizoid state described in Robert Laing's *Divided Self*.

> Ezekiel Mphahlele: 'I feel very gloomy about the situation as far as creative writing is concerned . . . Our energies go into this conflict to such an extent that we don't have much left for creative work. One might ask, "Why could this not be a spur towards creative writing?" I think it is paralysing. As writers, we build up ready, stock responses which always come out in our writing. Also cultural work in South Africa is so fragmented. We are in two ghettoes, two different streams, and you can't get really dynamic art in this kind of society. You won't get a great White novel, I think, and you won't get a great Black novel until we become integrated. As soon as the White man has learned to realize that he is an African and no longer a European, he will then begin to write an African novel or an African poem. Now, he still feels as part of Europe.'

II

I have tried to show, very sketchily, how apartheid promotes stagnation and splintering in all the different cultures it so idealistically set out to 'develop'. And I must insist that this is happening in spite of a natural trend to interact and to unite. I have said that culture implies that which distinguishes one society or nation from another. But it is true that the very nature of our world since the Second World War tends more and more towards international osmosis based on an

81

acknowledgement of the common humanity of all people. The Black Panther leader, Eldridge Cleaver, points out that *competition* is usually seen as one of the primary characteristics of humanity: his own interpretation of this impulse is that it represents the law of the jungle and that *co-operation* is the keyword of true civilization. It is interesting to note that Khruschev's phrase 'peaceful co-existence' has now been taken over by the National Party: its interpretation, however, is as much a travesty of the real meaning of the phrase as Khruschev's was: there is no real aim towards co-existence in an apartheid society: in the small isolated groups created by such a system each eventually excludes the other, distrusts the other, fears the other, and hates the other.

Within a few hours one can travel from any capital in the West to another; mass media tend to unite large portions of the world in common experiences; the exploration of the moon was universally experienced as a feat of *humanity*—not necessarily of Americans. The internationalization of sport creates new bonds. International programmes to combat famine, to explore the sea, to save water, to stop air pollution, etc. create an awareness of common goals. In the arts, the film has become the truly modern universal medium: the experiments of the avant-garde in Italy, America, Brazil, Poland or France reveal remarkable common denominators; the same is true of sculpture and painting and music; thanks to modern travel a Peter Brook production can travel to Czechoslovakia or the USA, and Grotowski can perform in London or New York; the Yanacek trio or I Musici can travel all over the world in a single season; and the Gonzales professional tennis team can compete in all countries. What happens in New York, or Tokyo, or Prague, or Sharpeville is of immediate relevance to all living persons. This has become startlingly clear in the course of student protests in Europe and America since 1967: the generation gap in our time is entirely different from that in any previous age, because of the international conscience that has come alive. A young demonstrator in Paris or Washington is not only *interested* in what happens in South Africa, but immediately *concerned* by it; it affects his personal future: because in our time Donne's words are more true than ever before: *No man is an island entire of itself* . . . We have the same goals and the same agonies; we are threatened by the same Bomb and tantalized by the same Space. The barriers in the way of true internationalism are class and race; therefore it is imperative—for all people— that they should be broken down. And that is why South Africa runs like a sewer through the conscience of the world.

Cultural events in the rest of the world cannot but influence South Africa. *Hair* is familiar to almost every teenager in the country even though it is banned in South Africa. *Bonnie and Clyde*, though banned too, is as much of a reality to the young cinema-goer as *Romeo and Juliet*. This general cultural awareness is in conflict with our factual isolation and causes a growing frustration which may reach a danger point. It is a climate in which youthful revolt thrives. If the SABC bans the Beatles it is all the more reason for the younger generation to listen to them. Miriam Makeba is a favourite and admired figure in almost as many white South African homes as 'our' international opera star Mimi Coertze is. And the face of Che Guevara looks down on countless teenage beds in South Africa.

In other words, in spite of censorship and the deliberate isolationist aims of apartheid we are continually exposed to a cultural bombardment from all over the world. But also inside the country, among the different cultural groups, there are strong movements against isolation. At the moment these movements have little to do with culture, but they have cultural potential. In spite of all apartheid ideals the country cannot exist without the economic interdependence of all its groups; and it is surely unnecessary to refer again to the growing number of Africans in cities in spite of influx control and repatriation schemes (which exist, for the greater part, on paper only). The unparalleled economic boom also affects all groups, creating more contact, and more cultural awareness—more cultural needs—in the less privileged groups. More people have more money, and so more people have access to some of the products of culture, or else grow more impatient in their demands. This is as simple as a law of nature and, I think, as irrepressible. Apartheid creates more and more of a paradox, where enforced isolation of groups wars against natural and inevitable contact.

III

It is always easier to describe a situation than to suggest a remedy. But I think the evaluation I have tried to give also implies some possibilities of specific action which may either speed up the breakdown of apartheid, or—at the very least— prepare a climate of 'readiness' for full cultural growth once the system has been destroyed.

1. I do not believe in cultural boycotts: keeping books, plays and academics out of South Africa is counter-productive. If it has any faith in the persuasive value of ideas, the outside world should expose South Africans to them as much as possible rather than cut off the hands of those inside the country who need the weight of revolutionary ideas to reinforce their own struggle for change. On economic boycotts there is simply too much contradictory evidence at this stage to make an unequivocal decision. But about the value of sports boycotts as a means of pressing for change in South Africa there can be little doubt. Recent events on the sports front all point in this direction. However revealing it may be of the cultural and spiritual adolescence of South Africans as a whole and the Afrikaner in particular, the fact remains that sport is one of apartheid's most vulnerable areas. It is true that opposition, protest marches overseas and isolation locally sometimes appeal to the masochistic sentiments of—especially—Afrikaners and may increase

their determination to 'stand firm'. At the same time such people find it difficult to swallow the fact that at a moment when on so many fronts South African sports are flourishing we should be isolated. I feel more specific use should be made of top sportsmen to denounce the system or to plead for change. A few isolated cases are not good enough. Both the American Establishment and Black Power leaders have long ago realized how necessary it is to use figures with mass appeal in their campaigns: even presidential elections are run with the aid of comedians, film stars or jazz singers. A definite effort can be made to co-ordinate widespread dissatisfaction in sports circles and deliberately to provoke showdowns if necessary. It is not enough to have convictions; one should be prepared to do something about them. It is no use simply to say that one is against something: it should be proved by acts. Also, a definite programme of 'education' can be put into practice to reveal, bluntly and sensibly, to the ordinary mass of readers of any magazine or newspaper *why* students and other people overseas protest against the Springboks and other South African sportsmen. It was remarkable to note the effect of a single letter from an Afrikaans student at Oxford who explained why he took part in the demonstrations: obviously many people turned violently against him, but a significant number were impressed, and at least started thinking about the 'whys'. If this letter had been followed up by others it could have become much more useful. Here, as in all other cultural fields, it seems to me that co-ordination is an absolute necessity. It is specifically necessary that more such 'revelations' should come from Afrikaners. Because the whole situation in this country places the Afrikaner in a position where his criticism has more weight than that of anyone else: after all, by virtue of the colour of his skin and by virtue of his language, he is a member of the Establishment.

2. This is equally true in the arts. The best proof is the Breytenbach syndrome. For purely private reasons Breytenbach married the Vietnamese woman he loved and

quite unexpectedly found himself in the midst of a furore when he was awarded a literary prize only to find out that he could not come home to collect it because his wife, though whiter than many Afrikaners, was non-white in the eyes of the law. This incident forced a non-political person into the political arena. In a devastatingly logical way he developed his political philosophy to the point where he had to attack the country in public. And now he will refuse to return, even if he were allowed to do so, unless all his non-white co-exiles can return too: for why should an exception be made of him because he happens to be white, and Afrikaans?

The point of Breytenbach's position is this: he is indeed one of the greatest poets Afrikaans literature has yet produced; but what makes him *politically* relevant is that to an overwhelming majority of people who have never read a single line of his verse, he has become a symbol of resistance to oppression. To many Africans, coloureds and Indians he has given new hope: because of his marriage and because of his convictions. As a result, every line of poetry he writes—even if it is the purest lyrical verse—acquires *political* implications. Many of the younger generation of Afrikaners react to him as others do to Guevara. The publication of his latest volume *Kouevuur* is a deliberate act of defiance, not just because of its contents, but simply because he has written it, and published it in South Africa. And much of his particular impact is due to the fact that he is an Afrikaner. Again, in other words, we should realize that this is a function of cultural leaders which can be activated to help bring apartheid down. I have said that many Afrikaans writers still condone apartheid. Yet they are also dissatisfied with much of the iniquity perpetrated by the regime. This dissatisfaction can be harnessed and used. Ideally one should like to see the emergence of Afrikaans novels of considerable merit published which expose the whole terrible truth of the South African system. But one cannot 'demand' anything of a writer: if he writes to order, it may well be rubbish. What can be relevant, however, is the position of the writer in society—simply by virtue of the fact that *he is a writer*. Millions of people all over the world have been inspired by Solzhenitsyn's example without reading a word of his work.

3. Perhaps a South African writers' congress can be arranged: it should not be too difficult to find an international sponsor. Ideally this congress should be attended by writers from all groups in the country—including those in exile. For that reason it may have to be held in Swaziland or another neighbour state. If such a congress, with several leading Afrikaans writers attending, can come out strongly against the cultural sterility caused by apartheid and insist on the solidarity of writers irrespective of race or language it may have an effect: not necessarily in immediate, practical terms, but in the process of bringing the country to an awareness of what is really going on.

4. It should be clear from the above that a programme similar to that of Brazil's *conscientizacão* can be of great value here. This may take the form of small cultural groups established all over the country, and across all racial barriers, to work together on cultural projects. In Bloemfontein an Afrikaans actor brought together a coloured group and embarked on a theatre programme. In Grahamstown a group is now being established to work towards the production of something like Peter Brook's *US*, but with apartheid as its theme: the aim is to develop into an interracial group. This can also be done in the form of debating societies, literary discussion groups, writing workshops, amateur theatre groups, music groups, 'folk' groups all aimed at cultural integration. One should at all costs avoid an impression of cultural missionary work, which would be as odious as organized charity. These groups do not exist to 'dispense' anything: they want to create something communally. This can be co-ordinated with a purely educational programme for Africans, along Brazilian lines: not only to supplement the scant and slanted teaching of Government schools but

specifically to teach people what they do *not* learn at school.

5. Censorship plays a large part in maintaining cultural backwardness: so censorship must be attacked. It is not enough to denounce it: many have done so to no avail. Censorship must be attacked frontally. I should suggest that several leading authors and/or academics—including as many Afrikaners as possible—deliberately seek prosecution for possessing banned books: preferably those books by the world's leading writers and philosophers. These writers (of whom I am most willing to be one) must refuse to pay fines and choose to go to jail. If only five are prepared to do so in conjunction, the impact will be very great. The law may not be changed. But something in the climate will change; a narrowing in a certain group, but also a widening in another. Obviously this must not be done for the sake of facile martyrdom! But it can be an effective act—in the long run.

6. At one performance of Fugard's *Boesman and Lena* before a coloured audience in the Luxurama, a teacher came to Fugard and said: 'I want you to know that we laughed because we thought we ought to. If we'd started to cry, we wouldn't have been able to stop.' And during the performance of *People are living there*, when one character on stage accused the other of hiding behind his white skin, the entire audience jumped to their feet and shouted: 'Yes!'

In a society where this can happen, theatre is an electric medium. In Europe and England, where reflexes have become stale, the theatre is dying—unless it is resurrected in new forms like the theatre of cruelty, living theatre, etc. But in South Africa theatre *has something to say*. It is the most social of all arts. And it can be encouraged to fulfil its social function more fully. Even within the framework allowed by the Regional Arts Councils, much of significance can be accomplished. For the rest, amateur groups can be cultivated to produce a truly social 'theatre of revolt'.

7. Much can be done with films, too, although censorship is extremely rigid. There is a growing number of young actors

and film technicians eager to experiment with this exciting medium: this can be put to a socio-cultural use to shock people in this country into awareness of what is really being done to human beings in the name of Christian apartheid. Even great cultural and social revolutions begin with basic moral questions in the consciences of a few.

One should not be discouraged by the lack of a favourable 'climate'. Climates can be stimulated, or even created. It is not a question of quantity, but of quality.

8. In the minds of many people the Afrikaans language is associated with the apartheid Establishment. This could lead to cultural tragedy. Consequently it becomes imperative that Afrikaans writers should be made more aware of the enormous social responsibility they have to bear in addition to their normal human conscience as writers. *They have to prove to the world that the Afrikaans language can—and must—be something different from the language of apartheid.*

9. A purely semantic matter may seem out of place here, yet I believe it has considerable significance. Among Afrikaners, even progressive ones, there is a strange persistence in referring to blacks as *kaffirs*; many English, even of a liberal persuasion, talk about the *boys* or *girls* in their employ, even if these persons are older than the speakers. The very fact that some well-meaning people are not even aware of the offensiveness of such terms is revealing. In 'a purely semantic matter' is expressed the essence of the South African tragedy: that most whites have simply not yet begun to think of blacks as *human beings*.

A word like *kaffir*, *Bantu*, *boy* or *girl* is a denial of the human individuality of another person (as American soldiers talk of Gooks and Viets—until they have so dehumanized the 'enemy' that they can massacre women and children). It should be a simple, but remarkably effective, remedy consciously to propagate the use of the words 'man', 'woman' and 'child' for anybody in this country, irrespective of colour. In situations where, for some reason, it is absolutely

89

unavoidable to distinguish colour (and I think one will discover that there are surprisingly few such situations), it should be easy to refer to a black man or a white woman or brown child.

IV

We live in a dissatisfied country, an unhappy country, a violent and tragically splintered country. But basically we all belong here—and nowhere else. There are enormous differences between us, but all differences can eventually be eliminated consciously by starting out from a position of love and understanding And love and understanding can emerge from cultural maturity. This can arise from a true interaction of indigenous and foreign cultures. One need never assume that another person is in all ways similar to oneself, blinding oneself to differences. But it can be fatal to see another as so completely different from oneself that one denies not only his or her humanity but one's own. I believe that on the road this country has chosen we are heading for a violent explosion. But I also believe that it can still be avoided—not by evasion or illusion, but by creative preparation. The very unrest and dissatisfaction so evident all round us can be moulded into creativity in order to arrive finally at a truly vital South African culture.

Postscript (1982)

In many respects the South African scene has changed during the twelve years since this article was written. The question, of course, is whether these changes are significant or merely 'interesting'.

1. Many hotels, theatres and restaurants in the country have opened their doors to customers other than white,

initially by way of an extensive permit system, nowadays with a less obtrusively bureaucratic approach. Removing 'Whites Only' notices in Post Offices and other public buildings has not resulted in bloodshed and revolution. On television, white viewers have become used to seeing blacks in roles of social and moral equality and sometimes superiority. To the young generation of Afrikaners skin colour is no longer an automatic indication of class distinction as it was in my own youth. A process of historical evolution—Nkosi's 'natural impulse'—has been eroding the rigidities of apartheid as an all-embracing system. This has been aided by the slow emergence of a black middle class which is, in fact, encouraged by the authorities. And since the eruption of Soweto in 1976 the Government has been forced, albeit reluctantly, to pay more attention to the opinions of leaders from other population groups and to the demands of black trade unions.

Yet one should be careful not to interpret these changes as a dismantling of apartheid. As long as the cornerstones of the ideology remain intact—Group Areas, including the splintering of the country into a chequered map of 'homelands' and a staggering programme of resettlement; separate education systems; the 'Immorality' Act; an entire economy based on exploitation—apartheid will persist. What we have seen in recent years has been a modernizing, a sophistication of the system; by no means a development towards its radical destruction.

2. A particularly spectacular development has taken place, as a direct result of international pressure and boycotts, in the integration of sports in South Africa. In many instances it is still restricted to tokenism, as in rugby; other sports, like boxing and soccer, have become almost completely non-racial. It has reached a stage where many South Africans, especially 'well-meaning' ones, are pained by the fact that in spite of such changes the country is not yet readmitted to many fields of international competition: they protest very

strongly against the politicization of sport. The point is, of course, that South Africa itself was one of the first countries to politicize sport (in fact, to politicize every aspect and facet of human existence, including the most private); and having discovered the peculiar power of sport in the South African context as a means of exerting pressure for change, not just in sport itself, and not just superficial or symbolic in nature and extent, the world would be foolish to abandon this one lever it has been using so effectively. After all, what has to be changed in the country is not the rules allowing people of different colours to kick or hit the same ball, but the very foundations on which this society rests, and of which playing ball is only a minor symptom. Since sport has proved to be an Achilles heel in the body of apartheid, this form of pressure should be used until the whole organism is destroyed.

3. Education in South Africa has undergone some promising changes, notably after Soweto. More efforts are made today to raise the deplorable standards of black education; and at tertiary level a trickling of black students into white universities has become noticeable. It may well acquire its own historical momentum and eventually break down the insulting barriers not only between different population groups but between people and learning, people and knowledge. However, for as long as the Government refuses to accept a single education system for all races—as recommended in 1981 by its own De Lange commission— this will remain one of the danger points in the country. It certainly is a territory where increasing pressure for cultural change should be exerted; and it seems to me that universities can play a major role in establishing a proper basis for such development. The possibilities, however small, have been created. What is now required is sustained and unremitting pressure.

4. Although it does not fall entirely within the scope of this article, it seems to me much more can be done about activating the Church itself as a factor for change. Ever since

its inception apartheid has been allowed to determine the fate of South Africans mainly because a political system has consistently relied on the Dutch Reformed Churches for moral and religious justification. With the growing unrest in Afrikaans theological circles it seems likely that this central pillar may be crumbling, which may bring the whole Temple of Dagon crashing down on the Philistines. The expulsion of the Afrikaans churches from the international community of Protestants (and the election of a charismatic young coloured theologian, Dr Alan Boesak, as international president of the World Alliance of Reformed Churches) will inevitably encourage greater internal polarization: a vicious Rightist backlash versus, hopefully, a more open, more humane, in fact more Christian approach. And this in itself can become another growth point for significant cultural change in general.

5. Specifically in the field of writing some of the most truly significant changes have come about. At the time of writing my article in 1970, I was deeply concerned about two aspects in particular: the cultural schizophrenia of Afrikaans writers, and the separateness of different literatures in the country. In both respects the situation has developed quite remarkably in the course of the 1970s.

Realizing the limitations they have imposed on themselves by trying to bring about a revolution in aesthetics only, with strong moral and religious undertones, at least a few Afrikaans writers have followed the pioneer Jan Rabie into accepting the full political implications of writing in a restricted society. As a result, their approach has become more and more identified with South Africa, Africa and the Third World rather than with Europe. This did not result in parochialism which had been the fate of most Afrikaans fiction prior to the 1960s. On the contrary, much of this recent work appears to stand a greater chance than before of breaking through international barriers precisely because it does not 'compete' with the work of other, Western, writers but offers something essentially African. In a profound way it also implies a solidarity with the essential experience of the Afrikaner himself, as a creature and a progeny of this continent. Understandably, the conflict with the Afrikaner Establishment has persisted, has even increased: but it no longer alienates the writer, because in his work he has finally come to terms with what is most profound in himself. We have at last *come home*.

This, and also the awareness of a common enemy, has inspired greater solidarity among all writers in the country, irrespective of race or language (cf. the essay 'English and the Afrikaans Writer'). A particularly rewarding and illuminating experience was the establishment of a PEN Centre in Soweto late in the 1970s, in which writers from all language groups worked together. Sadly, the organization was short-lived, mainly as a result of pressure on black writers by their community which rejects all signs of collaboration. The important fact, however, it seems to me, is that although the organization itself has fallen victim to apartheid in this way, close personal relationships established among writers of different races persist in a rewarding and stimulating manner.

6. Censorship became immeasurably worse after this article was first written; at last it turned on Afrikaans writing as well and having done so, subjected Afrikaans authors to a worse reign of terror than that our English compatriots had become used to. One of the results was a severe inhibition of Afrikaans writing during the 1970s; but at least some authors refused to be intimidated and went on to challenge the regime with each new book. And after the censors had overstepped an imaginary line with the banning of a novel by Etienne Leroux and thereby inviting the vociferous opposition of the Afrikaans literary establishment itself, the administration of censorship took a new turn and since 1979 became in many respects more liberal, suggesting something of an uneasy Prague Spring. (This is discussed at some length in 'Censorship and Literature'.)

In the process, works previously relegated to the drawer finally saw the light of day: Breytenbach's *Om te Vlieg* was published in 1971; Rabie's *Agitator* was revised and published in 1977 as *Ark*; my own *Saboteurs* was abandoned in its original form, but parts of it were resuscitated in *Looking on Darkness* (1974) and *Rumours of Rain* (1978). The poems excised from Breytenbach's *Kouevuur* were published in a small private edition in 1971, and a few of them were later incorporated in a selection of his work (1977).

This does not mean that South Africa has really made significant progress on the way towards that radical and profound change of attitude as well as of structures which alone can guarantee a more liveable future for all the inhabitants of the country. In many ways, in fact, the overall situation appears more gloomy than ever before. If the questioning and soul-searching in Afrikaner circles has assumed greater proportions than before, a reactionary movement to the Right has also become much more evident: and with the Government caught in this cleft stick indications are that pusillanimity and lack of vision may determine their choice.

The very gravity of the situation, however, suggests that pressures within the field of culture should be increased rather than abandoned or lessened. For culture is involved with attitudes, mental processes, sympathies, modalities, awareness: and this remains the nerve-centre, and even the condition, of any truly significant change in other areas, including the political.

English and
the Afrikaans Writer

(1976)

> It is as if the aspiring young writer, including the
> Afrikaans writer, were told: 'If you have something to
> say, my boy, then write in English! And if you don't
> know English well enough, then learn it like Joseph
> Conrad: but write in English and save your soul!'
>
> *N. P. Van Wyk Louw*

I

English has always played an important role in the world of
the Afrikaans writer, ever since some of the earliest forms of
written Afrikaans made their appearance in the work of
English writers (cf. Andrew Geddes Bain's *Kaatje Kekkelbek* in
1846). At the time of the First Language Movement, from
1875 onwards, English was experienced as the language of
the oppressor (C. P. Hoogenhout: "Tis English, English,
nought but English; English that one sees and hears. /In our
schools and in our churches 'tis the slaughter of our
tongue . . .'), but the real struggle at that stage was with
Dutch. The fight with English was a form of open,
conventional warfare involving two different groups, two
separate cultural identities; the fight with Dutch was more

intimate and obscure, a fierce civil war with guerilla tactics. English was a material and political threat, but Dutch jeopardized the very *raison d'être* of Afrikaans by humiliating it as a 'kitchen language', an inferior and largely unwritten patois.

Many of the pioneers of Afrikaans literature were prepared to write in English when it suited them; but not in Dutch. In a very real sense Dutch had become an utterly foreign language within the Cape context (in the Transvaal it was kept alive, artificially, through the wiles and stubbornness of President Kruger). And after nearly a century of British rule English, however much resented as the language of the oppressor, had become a window on the world—whereas Dutch, except in Church circles maintaining strong ties with Holland, was almost irrelevant.

This may account, to some extent, for the special love-hate relationship between Afrikaans and English once the battle against Dutch had been won: English, as a great and established world language, was experienced as a threat to the survival of the small new language which had so precariously taken root locally; but at the same time it provided a means of communication with the entire outside world. And it is significant that the staunchest chauvinist in the struggle for Afrikaans and one of the most untiring pioneers in the establishment of literary tradition, C. J. Langenhoven, had for many years championed the cause of English as the sole official language of the country, before taking up the cudgels for Afrikaans.

Several poets from the first generations of Afrikaans writers in the twentieth century wrote much of their work in English. Eugène Marais made his debut as a poet in English before publishing, in 1905, what is now generally acknowledged to be the first wholly successful Afrikaans lyric; and several of his major contributions to non-fiction during his more mature years were also in English (including *The Soul of the Ape*).

Louis Leipoldt, who, like Marais, spent several years of

study and research in Britain, often claimed that all his poetry was originally written in English and then translated—a dubious claim he is alleged to have maintained until someone once challenged him actually to quote a couple of lines from one of his lyrics in English.

Even early writers who wrote exclusively in Afrikaans revealed the influence of English on their work: there is more than a dash of Scott in J. H. H. de Waal, even though his primary inspiration must have been the Dutch novelist Van Lennep; and much of Jan Celliers's *Die Vlakte* derives from Shelley's *Cloud*, via Jacques Perk. And this, really, became indicative of the relationship between Afrikaans writing and English literature for many years: if English was practically never employed in the writing of Afrikaans authors during the decades between the two World Wars it remained a stimulus, often a source of inspiration. Even when that inspiration was derived from works in other languages, like French, English often served as the vehicle to convey the original. Let it be said, however, that the Afrikaans writer has traditionally been a rather formidable linguist, exploring a variety of other literatures, from Greek and Latin to Italian and German, in the original. One of the results of this activity has been the veritable epidemic of translations from other languages to appear in Afrikaans—a phenomenon which seems to be characteristic of other more or less geographically restricted languages like Finnish, Icelandic, Swedish, Danish and Norwegian. If there have been comparatively fewer works translated from English into Afrikaans than from languages like French or German, this must be ascribed to the obvious fact that English is already accessible to most Afrikaans readers.

II

Two extreme tendencies emerged in the course of the 1930s. On the one hand there was an increasing sense of linguistic purism, degenerating into puritanism: an exaggerated and often ridiculous fear of English influences on Afrikaans, resulting in a witch-hunt to eradicate all anglicisms from the language—an activity prompted by very real fears at the outset, but persisting much longer than was necessary, eventually threatening the Afrikaans language itself with impoverishment and undernourishment. Today this attitude survives mainly as a symptom of political (extreme Right) conviction, but originally the aims were laudable and positive enough—namely to avoid the 'easy way out' in trying to cope linguistically with new challenges; and, instead of simply borrowing solutions from English, the syntactic, semantic and morphological possibilities of Afrikaans itself were explored. But even then the results were often curiously negative. The works of Sangiro (a noted writer of animal and nature stories), for example, were widely praised—and as widely prescribed in schools—because they were found to be 'wholly free of anglicisms'. That they abounded in germanisms, and that major portions were in fact plagiarized from German, did not seem to bother anyone.

At the other extreme, it happened for the first time that an Afrikaans writer started writing, with equal facility and equal felicity, in both Afrikaans and English, as a matter of free choice, and not as a result of background (as in the case of Leipoldt and Marais) or politics (as in the case of Langenhoven). The writer in question is, of course, Uys Krige. There is something of a consistent procedure in Krige's writing of poetry and drama, which usually is done first in Afrikaans and translated subsequently, sometimes with an interval of decades; but his choice of a language medium for prose seems arbitrary. Some of his best work has been written in English first (*The Way Out*, 'Death of a Zulu'), but at least an equal amount in Afrikaans. What is of particular significance is that, with Krige, the Afrikaans and English texts are never absolutely identical. There is very little evidence of 'translation' in the ordinary sense of the word: in every instance the 'translation' becomes a re-thinking, a recasting of the original in terms of the medium of the new language.

And where languages differ as radically, especially syntactically, as Afrikaans and English, this leads to variations worthy of closer analysis. In Krige's short stories, or non-fiction narratives, especially, the difference between Afrikaans and English narrative tenses creates notable and often exciting temporal shifts. In his poetry the translated version is invariably longer than the original (whether the poem in question is one of his own or one of, say, Lorca's; even his magnificent rendering of *Twelfth Night* contains the characteristic and brilliant 'Krige cadenzas'); in his plays the translated version is—surprisingly!—often drastically shortened. In every case there is, obviously, a thematic resemblance; but the rendering in the new language bears witness of a thorough re-experience of the basic material. And it often happens that, after translating a given text, the original is also revised—amounting, effectively, to a re-translation from the first translated form. This is especially notable in Krige's one-act plays, first written in Afrikaans, then rewritten in English, and finally recomposed in Afrikaans.

In the course of the 1930s Uys Krige was unique in this respect, and in many ways he remains unique within the context of the whole of Afrikaans literature. But it is significant that at least one of his contemporaries, Elisabeth Eybers, has also developed into a skilful and highly sensitive translator of her own poems into English. In addition, she occasionally produces a poem exclusively in English—all the more remarkable for a poet living, for the past decade and more, in voluntary exile in Holland.

III

Since the Second World War it has been happening increasingly—although it is by no means a common phenomenon yet—that works by Afrikaans writers become available in English: either in translations by others (Chris Barnard, Etienne Leroux), or in their own translations (Jan Rabie, W. A. de Klerk). An author like De Klerk, who spent several years in Britain immediately after the War, has also started publishing directly in English (his *Puritans in Africa*), but only non-fiction, and for all too obvious reasons of a mainly political nature. Among the younger poets there appear to be several who write equally well (or, in some cases, equally badly) in Afrikaans and English. And there are others, among whom Wopko Jensma is the most notable, who use the vernacular of the black townships in a hotchpotch of africanized Afrikaans and English in which, in its most inspired moments, one seems to recognize the stirrings of an altogether new poetic language. This is evident also in recent poetry by black poets like Sipho Sepamla.

IV

Historically, then, the importance of English for the Afrikaans writer, not only as a source of inspiration but also as a form of expression, can be established without any problem. More important, when surveying the contemporary scene, is the emergence of a climate anticipated in a certain sense by Van Wyk Louw's famous anti-censorship letter to *Die Burger* in 1963, a portion of which was quoted as a motto for this article:

> At a recent prize-giving ceremony I happened to find myself in the proximity (spiritually at least) of a compatriot who writes in English. She publishes her

books abroad and apparently earns good money with them; no South African censorship can touch her (it may even be to her advantage!); she can bring her royalties into South Africa from all over the world and the government will welcome this 'influx of capital'. It occurred to me: She can ignore our censorship. But what about me and my Afrikaans colleagues? We shall have to try and bow under this yoke. Or . . . ?

I doubt whether even Lord Milner could have devised a more effective way of hamstringing Afrikaans and allowing English a free rein. It is as if the aspiring young writer (including the Afrikaans writer) were told: 'If you have something to say, my boy, then write in English! And if you don't know English well enough, then learn it like Joseph Conrad: but write in English and save your soul!'

Truly, as an Afrikaner who has never made a secret of his Afrikaner nationalism, either here or abroad, I find it impossible to grasp the motive which could have seduced a Nationalist government into formulating a Bill of such dubious 'morality' and so utterly anti-Afrikaans.

It seems to me that two sets of factors operate in the present situation. One of them, censorship, as viewed by Louw, is negative: using English as a form of survival. But the other is positive: turning to English to complement the experience lived in Afrikaans, and vice versa. It becomes a dual exploration, a bifocal vision, of a single experience—that of living in (South) Africa.

In order to appreciate this, more is required than a simple historical survey. For in order to find an answer to the question: *Why should an Afrikaans writer write in English?* it is first necessary to ask: *Why write in Afrikaans?*

V

At first sight, of course, it seems a question so obvious as to be slightly ridiculous. After all, any writer uses the language which comes most naturally to him. In the majority of cases this is the language with, and within, which he grew up. When his environment, including his linguistic environment, changes it often provides a stimulus to explore the sound-memories of his mother tongue even more acutely than before: Breyten Breytenbach or Lawrence Durrell did not start writing in French after they had given up the countries of their birth. But in some cases writers did have to start writing in the language of their new environment, usually when they had no hope of communicating with their previous societies any more, or no interest in doing so. And so a Joseph Conrad or a Vladimir Nabokov would emerge. Within the context of Afrikaans literature we have Jan van Melle who wrote his best work in Afrikaans, not in his native Dutch; and, especially, the flamboyant Peter Blum who left behind his German–French–Italian background to become one of the most brilliant, if short-lived, comets to streak through our poetic skies.

In countries where two or more languages are spoken, social, political or other conditions may prompt a writer from one language group to write in another language also accessible and more or less natural to him: both Maeterlinck and De Ghelderode were Flemish by birth and upbringing, yet both chose to write in French. Especially where the mother tongue is restricted, geographically or otherwise, there may be a strong tendency to use a world language for literary communication (most of the leading French or English writers from Africa would fall in this category), although, of course, the same situation may be a stimulus to promote the local language: after all, that was one of the central motives behind the emergence of national literatures in the Renaissance, or even as late as the nineteenth century (what Mistral did for Provençal is exactly what leading local writers have been trying to do for Afrikaans).

Within a society with a particularly strong and active group mystique, like the Afrikaner, the use of the mother tongue for literary expression would be even more obvious, even if it meant severely restricting one's readership. In return, there was—certainly until as late as the Second World War—the compensation of being held in especially high esteem by one's society. In Afrikaans circles the writer used to fulfil the time-honoured function of the *vates*—probably because, in the very beginning of the language struggle, the writers were also political or national leaders. Even writers decidedly 'different' in their political or moral or religious outlook (like Marais, who insulted Paul Kruger and became a morphine addict in a puritanical society; or the enigmatic Leipoldt with his highly unorthodox views on anything from wine to religion; or Toon van den Heever with his *mania blasphematoria* . . .) were not only tolerated but widely accepted and occasionally revered.

The clash of Van Wyk Louw with Verwoerd in the early 1960s, and the advent of the Sestigers at more or less the same time, brought a drastic change. Louw, always obscure and elitist in the eyes of the masses, had nevertheless acquired sufficient prestige as sage and soothsayer to remain 'acceptable', certainly in cultural circles. But the iconoclast Sestigers caused bewilderment, confusion and incredible hostility—all the more so for being supported by the majority of Afrikaans newspapers, the very organs which had traditionally been the champions of the national, or the Establishment's, 'cause'.

It had often happened in the past that Afrikaans writers castigated their people. Marais and Leipoldt did it, so did Van Wyk Louw. And they never hesitated to attack the Establishment: Van Wyk Louw wrote vicious poems against the 'oppressor' of the 1930s; W. E. G. Louw published a series of ranting sonnets against the 'renegade' General Hertzog (poems which, if written by a supporter of the (Black) South African Students' Organization today, might earn the writer a term in jail). But somehow it was 'all right'—either because the 'oppressor' was someone else, or, more likely, because everything was kept 'in the family'. The Sestigers were different. Most of them had gone through the crucible of longer or shorter sojourns in a society totally alien to their own, namely Paris. This experience had become the main common denominator among them: essentially an experience of existentialist agony; of being forced to re-examine everything previously taken for granted, including one's own identity, one's history, one's links with one's community. Where the physical alienation from South Africa coincided with upheavals like that caused by Sharpeville, the experience became even more acute. And when these young writers returned to 'their own people' it resulted in violent clashes and misunderstandings. The more desperately they wanted to 'belong', in a traditional sense, the more rejected they were made to feel because of their 'difference'—but this in turn proved intensely stimulating and creative. Essentially they were torn between different sets of forces: Europe (through the existential nature of their experience and their self-discovery) and Africa (through the nature of their language); the local and the universal; the group and the individual.

The important thing was that they all wanted to write in Afrikaans. Which was not as easy as it might sound, for by then their spiritual environment had changed so radically as to become almost 'uncontainable' in Afrikaans. On the most basic level, Afrikaans simply lacked an adequate vocabulary to express the essential existential experiences; to say nothing of a vocabulary for the expression of (sexual) love. It had to be invented, remade, adapted. In an effort to explain the great efficacy of his translation of *Twelfth Night* Uys Krige suggested that Afrikaans, today, found itself at the same stage of development as Elizabethan English. And

105

certainly this experience of the youth and virility, the malleability of this young language has been one of the most exhilarating aspects about writing in Afrikaans. Every sentence, to us, became a journey of exploration. Every page we wrote was also a mapping of wild and new territories: not only in terms of the experience expressed, but primarily in terms of *language*.

And this, I think, provides the most important clue towards an answer to our question: *Why write in Afrikaans?*

It is an answer which lies in the intrinsic 'genius' of the language itself. The Dutch came to Africa with a variety of dialects at a crucial stage of development and were forced into the melting-pot of a wholly new environment, subject to all sorts of extraneous and internal influences—and gradually a new language emerged, adapted to the needs of this new, African situation. A view held by more and more linguists today is that, in fact, the Afrikaans language emerged from the efforts of non-Dutch speakers to speak Dutch in an African environment. Hence the very development of the language implied a dimension of the exploration of the African experience, a process intrinsic to the language itself.

In the suprematist terms of his age Langenhoven praised Afrikaans as 'the only white-man's language to be made in this country and not imported, ready-made, from overseas'. Of course, this also suggests an inherent restriction: Afrikaans, when it was consciously promoted as a language, was essentially African by nature (in the sense of being shaped in, for, and out of Africa), but it was not African in the same way as, say, Zulu or Xhosa or Swahili. It was a 'white' language (even though this appellation ignores the incalculable contribution especially of the coloureds towards its shaping and its growth). It was, in other words, a political instrument. And *at the time* that was an integral part of its very strength, and one of the main reasons why it eventually established itself as an officially recognized language.

The early writers in Afrikaans experienced the joy and wonder of exploring and expressing themselves, their time and their land in a language not yet formalized but in all respects adaptable to the requirements of their experience. Inasmuch as many of them were not (yet) good craftsmen, many or most of their efforts turned out to be literary failures. But as their craftsmanship improved—and as their tools were shaped and honed—a literature evolved which proved an exciting and wholly satisfying blend of the European and the African experience.

That is why most Afrikaans writers have found it impossible to write in anything but Afrikaans. English still proved too 'European', often as remote from the realities of the African experience as Dutch or German, whereas wholly indigenous languages like Zulu or Xhosa lacked the European dimension which, for white writers, continued to form a vital part of their experience.

Now it should also become evident why certain Afrikaans writers did manage to use English as a medium of expression parallel to Afrikaans: Uys Krige, for so many years a wanderer, a 'migratory bird', emotionally tied to his people yet temperamentally a loner, explored all the musical possibilities of Afrikaans—but also found it quite natural to switch to English when writing about experiences abroad, or about experiences with a broader human content. Elisabeth Eybers began to experiment with English after she left South Africa; De Klerk did so when he felt ostracized by his 'people' and welcomed by English speakers. Much of this last situation would seem to apply to the Sestigers too; surely, the liberating effect of their Parisian ecstasies and agonies made world languages more accessible to them.

Yet their first impulse was to turn to Afrikaans. (Even Jan Rabie who, during his seven years in Paris, had almost all the short fictions that were collectively entitled *21* published in English first. Breytenbach, on the other hand, during fifteen years of voluntary exile in Paris, did not write a single word in any language but Afrikaans.) For them to turn to English, something else had to happen: something had to occur within South Africa, and English itself had to be revealed in a new light.

VI

The English language that arrived at the Cape at whatever date one might care to choose—1875, 1803 or 1820—was altogether different from the conglomeration of Dutch dialects in 1652. Naturally all languages continue to change and develop; but the English transplanted to the Cape was undeniably a language already largely formalized and structured: whatever changes may have occurred since then have made little difference to the basic semantic, morphological and syntactic systems and processes of the language, and (apart from minor problems with accent) the Londoner of today has very little trouble in understanding English as she is spoke in South Africa. (Whereas Dutch literary reviews, with a highly erudite readership, are reluctant to publish any material in Afrikaans unless accompanied by a Dutch translation.)

Moreover, while the majority of the British Settlers of 1820 were from the lower classes the very nature of the South African economic situation soon established English as a *bourgeois* language on the continent. (Afrikaans, on the other hand, retained its working-class connections until at least the Second World War.) It was, in fact, as difficult for the English language to adapt to Africa in the nineteenth century as it would have been for a gentleman in top hat and tails to adjust to life in the bush. Adapt and adjust it did, let there be no doubt about that—and the current renaissance of English literature in South Africa provides splendid confirmation of the fact—but for a very long time, it seems to me, the nature of the language itself acted as a deterrent in the evolution of a significant indigenous literature. It seems almost incredible, in retrospect, that *The Story of an African Farm* could evoke, in 1883, so convincingly the essential African-ness of Olive Schreiner's experience: and her achievement is all the more remarkable if compared with what followed during the next half-century or so—a period when, with a handful of notable exceptions, English writers in South Africa seemed interested in the land only for what colour it could provide, with a number of misspelt *kopjes, sjamboks, veldtschoens* or *Vrouw Grobbelaars* thrown in for good measure. And it was the language as such which stood in the way—at least until the triumvirate of the magazine *Voorslag* (*Whiplash*), Roy Campbell, William Plomer and Laurens Van der Post effected an emancipation of South African English from its colonial bonds.

During the 1930s a remarkable reconnaissance of the country started, expressed in a language more fully shaped to the needs of the situation. And out of that venture, via the great contribution of Herman Charles Bosman (himself, like Van der Post, an Afrikaner writing exclusively in English), Alan Paton and others, emerged a vital and viable new literature bearing the paradoxical stamp of art in being both utterly local and utterly universal in its exploration of man in space and time.

Today, it appears to me—and I can as yet attempt only a tentative statement about it—a most interesting situation has come about. In the past, most Afrikaans works seemed more or less untranslatable into English (and an anthology like *Afrikaans Poems with English Translations* proved the point), and vice versa. I know from experience that it is easier to translate from French or Spanish or German into Afrikaans than from English. Yet I have, with sweat and close to tears, attempted translations from the works of Graham Greene, Henry James, and even Lewis Carroll and Shakespeare. But I would hesitate to attempt Nadine Gordimer in Afrikaans, just as I would be reluctant to translate Van Wyk Louw into English: in dealing with the experience of living-in-Africa, the one is so quintessentially 'English', the other so 'Afrikaans' (which is intended as a compliment to both) that their remoteness from one another is increased by their contingency. And this goes for much of the best work written in Afrikaans and in South African English until quite recently.

But this situation appears to be changing, at least in the work of certain authors. If I read Stephen Gray's *Local Colour* or J. M. Coetzee's *Dusklands* the fact that both are written in English seems almost coincidental. If I were stopped in the middle of a passage and asked whether I was reading a book in English or Afrikaans I might have to check the text before I could be quite sure. The same goes for, say, an Afrikaans novel by John Miles. And I find it even more obvious in much of the poetry written in either language in the country today. The change must, at least to some extent, lie in the language itself. Yet there is nothing 'English' about John Miles's Afrikaans and nothing 'Afrikaans' about Coetzee's English. (And I am deliberately *not* choosing examples like Van der Post, Athol Fugard or Bosman where the syntactic patterns of Afrikaans are evident just below the surface; or some passages of Etienne Leroux which are obviously 'English' in inspiration.) So the major change must have occurred in what *surrounds* the language, in its framework of reference, its patterns of possibilities, semantic or otherwise. And this would imply that both languages have reached a point where they are now fully geared to the realities of Africa: both have become sufficiently africanized to cope with Africa. Both have roots in Europe, but both have chosen Southern Africa as their 'operational area'. If this is so—and at this stage I can offer it only as conjecture—it would explain why Afrikaans authors may find it more 'natural' at this stage than before to communicate not only in Afrikaans but in English as well.

110

VII

What makes it particularly interesting is that this should occur at the very stage when at least some Afrikaans writers are forced seriously to consider the possibility of switching languages anyway.

This is caused partly—but only partly—by censorship. Van Wyk Louw's sombre predictions about the disastrous effects of the 1963 Publications and Entertainments Act were not quite realized, perhaps for the very reason that he voiced them in time. During the decade following the introduction of censorship Afrikaans literature certainly lost some of its verve and boldness. The decade which had started with so much promise and excitement ended with something of a whimper. Yet the factual situation was that, initially, censorship did not hit Afrikaans literature as hard as English. (Political considerations probably decided the issue: however recalcitrant, the Afrikaans writer was still regarded by the authorities as 'one of us'.)

The turning point came with the 1974 banning of *Kennis van die Aand* (*Looking on Darkness*). At last, it seemed, Afrikaans writers had overstepped the limit; the old taboos against ostracizing 'one's own' no longer operated; and once that had happened, it became easier to repeat the destructive action. Within a year four more Afrikaans works were banned. Under the new Publications Act (1974) it has become abundantly clear that Afrikaans films are allowed much less scope than imported products: even innocuous swear-words can lead to bans. And it would appear that the same is becoming true of literature. I have the impression that the position of ten years ago has now been reversed and that English writers (always provided they are not black!) are allowed somewhat more freedom than their Afrikaans colleagues.

But censorship is only a symptom of a much larger evil. What, in the Language Movement of the nineteenth

111

century, proved to be the forte of Afrikaans (the fact that it was a political instrument) has now developed into an Achilles heel. For as the Afrikaner became politically dominant his language also began to bear the stamp of exclusiveness—namely of White Afrikaner Nationalist Calvinist exclusiveness.

At least two extreme reactions to this alarming and saddening situation are possible, with a whole spectrum of intermediary ones. The one is denial and escape: refusing to write in Afrikaans any longer, and turning to English as the only way out. This attitude seems to be exemplified by Adam Small who, after a brilliant beginning as an Afrikaans poet and dramatist, seems finally to have turned his back on the language. His latest work includes a volume of poetry in English, and an anthology of translations from Van Wyk Louw—both of which are atrocious. And yet: ' . . . if you don't know English well enough, then learn it like Joseph Conrad . . . !' If one's work is consistently threatened by banning, it might well become necessary for more writers than just Adam Small to turn to English. On the other hand, it would be sad—and unforgivably defeatist—to do so unless it became totally impossible to write or publish in Afrikaans. And that day has not yet come. In fact, I am convinced that if Afrikaans writers would act with enough conviction and resourcefulness, trying to stay at least one step ahead of censorship all the time, it may not become necessary to escape into English at all. After all, that would sign a final death sentence for the language.

The other extreme reaction to the threat of Afrikaans becoming an exclusive political language is the one adopted by most younger writers so far: and that is deliberately to expand the scope of the language to reveal and to prove that it *is* more than the shibboleth of a faction. It becomes a creative effort to substantiate what Van Wyk Louw rather ambitiously claimed in the 1930s, namely that there should be nothing, but nothing, which cannot be said in Afrikaans.

If in *such* a situation Afrikaans writers turn to English, in addition to their own language, it would not imply escape but a positive and creative act of exploration.

After all, the experience of the Sestigers (as of their predecessors in the poetry of the 1930s) did contribute much towards the 'opening up' of the language. If they did direct techniques and influences acquired elsewhere towards their journey of discovery inward—into themselves, into the land, into the language itself—they also brought about a measure of sophistication, of 'internationalization' in Afrikaans literature. Consequently it is only natural to look outward towards other reading publics and markets as well: if only, initially at least, to obtain a greater measure of objectivity in one's evaluation of the local scene.

VIII

For myself, English has offered, above all, the challenge of a new medium: a challenge to myself, to try and convey to a public remote from Africa something of my African experience; but also a test of and a challenge to the language. It started with *Kennis van die Aand*, where intrinsic motives (the urge to attempt 'saying' the novel in a new language medium) as well as extraneous ones (censorship) combined to create the challenge. It became, purely on the level of the creative process itself, one of the most revealing experiences of my life: not 'translating' the work, but rethinking it in the framework of a new language; even more important, perhaps, re-feeling it. It even underwent a change of title, to *Looking on Darkness*, indicative of the process involved. It helped me discover a lot about my own language—more than any translation I had attempted previously. It is remarkable, for example, what difference there exists between the 'loads' of emotional content the two languages can carry. Afrikaans, like French, appears to offer a much higher resistance to

113

overstatement; it is much more at ease with superlatives and emotions. In English the threshold of overstatement is reached much more readily; 'valid' emotionalism in Afrikaans soon becomes unbearable in English. And this is but one, obvious, illustration of how one is forced to 're-feel' a novel in a new medium.

The experiment was carried a step further in my next novel, *An Instant in the Wind*. Making notes during the year which preceded the actual writing of the book, I found that more than half of these preliminary thoughts came to me, quite spontaneously, in English. (This was probably influenced by the fact that I was working on *Looking on Darkness* during some of this time.) Since the novel deals, essentially, with two modes of experiencing Africa (expressed in terms of a journey undertaken, in 1750, by a white woman and a black man from the wilderness of the Cape hinterland back to civilization), it was interesting to see how far the planning of the book could be influenced by thinking in English when dealing with the white character and in Afrikaans when imagining the black slave. It was quite impossible to adhere to a completely mechanical procedure, of course; rigorous application of the rule might have killed the book in the bud. Yet it was remarkable to see to what extent the two languages spontaneously associated themselves with the two spheres of experience represented by the main characters.

The few preliminary passages written to get the 'feel' of the book, after sorting the notes, were all in English. But, probably conditioned by previous writing, when I actually sat down to write, it happened in Afrikaans. That was only the beginning, though. Using the first draft as a guide, the whole book was then reworked in English. In the process some episodes contained in the Afrikaans draft simply fell away; a couple of new ones emerged quite spontaneously. After completion of this draft I spent some time working on both: some of the new 'English' episodes were incorporated in the

Afrikaans text, but one or two—including what I regard as a most vital one—simply didn't 'work' in Afrikaans. (The opposite was also true in a few cases.) The novel was then completed in English—and from that text a final Afrikaans version was prepared. There are still differences between them, and to my mind there is nothing to be done about that: the novel exists in two languages, but each language imposed its own demands on the final shape of the work.

The same might conceivably happen if a painter were to produce a work in a range of reds and then repeat it in, say, shades of blue: I can well imagine that the different colours would impose their separate 'logics' on the respective works, even to the extent of demanding a variation in shapes and textures. And returning from that dual experience the painter will probably know more about red and blue than before: discovering much about the red through working in blue, and the other way round.

I write in English, but I can never be an English writer: I can never use English like Nadine Gordimer or Dan Jakobson or Alan Paton. Not only because they have lived in the language from birth, but because their use of it embodies a peculiar form of being, of being-in-Africa, being-in-English. The English I use must bear the weight of my Afrikaans, of my Afrikaansness, because only in that way can I be true to my experience of the world as it takes shape, and assumes or produces meaning, in the act of verbalization.

Literature and Offence

(1976)

I

In the beginning was not the word but a complexity of experience both private and social. Then came the word, as a personal expression or interpretation of, and response to, that experience, directed towards society. *Langue*; *parole*; meaning. And then, among other things, came censorship, as one of a large range of possible reactions from society (or 'on behalf of' society) to experience so verbalized. In order, therefore, to explore the intricate relationship between writer and society it would seem wise to start with that point of contact between them; the word; language.

At first sight there appears to be no essential difference between the writer's relationship with his medium and that of the sculptor with his marble, the painter's with his canvas and paints, or the composer's with his melodies. In each case the medium is taken from a larger 'natural' context in order to fulfil a new aesthetic function, or assume a new aesthetic shape *not* 'natural' or 'normal' to it. In its natural state marble exists as part of a mountain; even after it has been hewn nothing 'pre-destines' it for sculpture: it can be used for building or paving or in a score of other ways. The same applies to colour or sound, which exist freely in nature and

116

can function in contexts utterly different from that of the painter or the composer. Similarly, language is used universally in human society as a form of expression or communication which need not have anything to do with literature at all.

Yet this is an over-simplification, as literature differs from other art forms in at least two very important ways:

1. The sculptor, having removed his marble from its original context, does not return or restore his sculpture to the mountain; Beethoven may use the notes of the cuckoo in his Sixth Symphony and adapt the sounds of brook and storm and dancing peasants, but the audience of his composition are members of human society, not those creatures of nature that produced the material. The writer, on the other hand, uses his language medium to communicate with the very society which has provided him with it. He may, of course, choose to destroy his work or keep it locked up in his drawer, but by its very nature the process of writing cannot be regarded as complete before the work has entered into communication with society—in other words, before the 'work of art' has become, in Ingarden's terminology, an 'aesthetic object'.

2. The sculptor 'owes' nothing to the mountain and has no responsibility towards it other than, perhaps, some gratitude for having obtained his material from it. But the writer finds himself in a much more complex situation. Not only does society provide him with his very medium of interpretation or communication, but he himself is a product of that society. It is from this double relationship that so much of the confusion surrounding the 'place' or 'role' of literature in society is derived.

II

In the heart of this situation lies the fact that the writer uses

117

his language in a way—and directs it to an end—different from its ordinary functions in society. This difference is usually explained in terms of selection and refinement and is influenced, obviously, by the genre concerned: the poet uses the *verse* or *line* as the smallest autonomous component of his language construction, whereas the prose writer exploits the *full sentence* and the dramatist the *individual utterance* (whether a single sentence, a gesture or a whole soliloquy). And these units, although autonomous in the sense of being comprehensible on their own, all contribute towards the whole of the work in question and, in turn, derive their full meaning from that whole.

But apart from these well-known and almost 'technical' considerations, one might be justified in characterizing, with a certain amount of generalizing, certain tendencies in which the writer's use of language differs from that of society. It may be said, for example, that whereas society tends to enslave language the writer strives to liberate it. Society, by virtue of its very nature, must generalize and systematize language within a structure of acceptable common denominators: the writer must hone blunted words anew, rekindle the fire of 'original inspiration' in them, rediscover original meanings or discover new ones, departing in every respect from the well-known and well-trodden syntactical or semantic paths, exploring whatever territory remains unknown on either side.

What results from it, in practice, is that language in society tends to conceal, even to lie, whereas the writer uses it as an instrument in search of truth, which is essentially non-verbal (hence the tendency of writers, notably poets, to despair about the efficacy of the very medium which is their only means of communication). While the ladies of society cover themselves with the bones of dead whales and the furs of dead foxes, the writer performs a striptease.

III

The result is, inevitably, to a larger or lesser degree, friction or confrontation, some form of offence.

All significant art is offensive.

I hope to substantiate what, at first sight, might seem a sweeping statement of no mean presumption.

'Offend', 'offensive' is used here in the original sense suggested by the etymology of the word as it is given in *The Shorter Oxford English Dictionary*, namely 'OF. *offendre* to strike against . . . ' The element of resistance, of some form of obstacle is essential to the notion of offence. But this can, of course, cover a very wide spectrum of experience ranging from an aggressive reaction to what is felt as a real threat (for example to moral, religious, political or other convictions), to mild excitement upon being confronted by something novel and unfamiliar in a purely aesthetic situation (like an unexpected rhyme, or a new strategy among the 'codes' of fiction). If 'recognition' is an important attribute of the aesthetic experience it seems to me at least of equal importance for that recognition to be accompanied by, or clothed in, or arrived at, via an awareness of surprise: the aesthetic object does not communicate to its public in a purely passive state but only by dint of encountering, or arousing, and eventually overcoming an initial resistance. It is the breakthrough of the unfamiliar (or of the familiar in unfamiliar guise) into the domain of the familiar.

As an illustration one might use two examples of the short story. Imagine the reader as a man taking a nap at a picnic spot. Then O. Henry would crawl up to him and suddenly yell in his ear as loudly as possible, waking up the sleeper with a violent shock. In the same situation, Katherine Mansfield would approach as quietly, but she would pick a blade of grass and start tickling the sleeper with patient persistence until it penetrates his dreams and forces him to wake up. The result is the same: the sleeper has been awakened to a state of consciousness and seeing; and however great the difference between the approaches of the two authors, both have 'pushed' or 'struck against' an object, both have 'offended' the sleeper, both have broken through his resistance.

And essentially this offence is determined by the tension which exists between the writer's use of language and that of society: the difference, in other words, between the uniqueness of the experience of an individual (the writer), and his interpretation of that experience—and, on the other hand, society's acquiescence in traditional, conventional, stereotyped ways of looking, listening, thinking and experiencing.

From this initial situation an important aspect of the problem is derived: while the experienced reader is prepared to rid himself of personal prejudice in his more or less shocking confrontation with a work of art, in order to transcend the purely personal into an active state of awareness, the less experienced person remains trapped on the first—psychological—level of 'being offended'. Perceiving only the obviously 'offensive' elements in the situation he is unable to yield himself to the liberating experience which flows from unreserved communication— or even communion—with the work confronting him. (And so, when he demands to be 'protected' against such works it is basically himself he needs protection from.)

IV

The situation is further complicated, as I have suggested, by the fact that this communication does not take place in a void but within a more or less clearly definable cultural and social milieu. The Afrikaans novel is 'addressed to' the Afrikaans reader within a given context of values, traditions, concepts, taboos and prescripts—and this situation may reach the extreme where a work from one cultural context becomes nearly unintelligible to a person from a different culture, or to someone from the same culture but in a different historical context. (Why is Racine nearly always a failure when produced in English, or Shakespeare in French?)

When the conventional reader of an Afrikaans novel opens his book, he brings with him a complex world conditioned culturally, socially, politically, psychologically, even economically; in the widest possible sense and on the most banal level he expects that what is written in Afrikaans will also endorse his own 'Afrikaansness'. (And since this concept in itself is a matter of *tantes homines* . . . the problem becomes even more tricky.)

But, like the reader, the work also carries its own 'world' with it: the reader opening a novel or embarking upon the reading of a sonnet does so equipped with a whole set of anticipations and even presumptions determined by the mere mention of the name 'novel' or 'sonnet'. This conditioning will, of course, be determined by the extent of the reader's experience in literature, and in life: Chomsky's 'competence'. And as a result of the increasing ease with which modern communication media and transport create contact between different societies and cultures, the 'resistance level' in communities and individuals is constantly, and rapidly, changing.

The basic situation remains unchanged, however: however 'open' or 'sophisticated' a reader may be, he will always experience some form of 'offence' when confronted with a really significant work. That is one reason why some 'masterpieces' retain their importance through centuries while others simply disappear and yet others are miraculously 'rediscovered': they retain their faculty of 'offending' us, even though this 'offence' may operate for wholly different reasons, or in wholly different ways, from the initial experience. This explains much of the theatre work of, say, Jan Kott or Peter Brook with Shakespeare: rather than allow us to relax with a familiar text they use every effort to discover the essential 'offensiveness' of Shakespeare for the audiences of our own time. They must first discover—or even set up—a new range of resistance in order to break through to new levels of meaning.

V

The very 'literariness' of a text may be influenced by its offensive qualities. In spite of the assertions of great theoreticians like Sartre and Van Wyk Louw, the literary text, whether fiction or poetry, is *not* a transparent glass through which a 'world beyond' can be observed. The qualities of the glass itself—its opacity, thickness, coloration, convexity or concavity, its smoothness or otherwise— demand the attention of the spectator. The 'real' world enters into it, of course: the referential nature of language itself makes it inevitable. But in the final analysis it is the *density* of the literary experience which determines our way of looking 'through' it at the world beyond. If this were not so, if the world outside the work coincided perfectly with the one within it, the reader would be no more than a consumer, a receiver of messages, a decoder of pre-existent meaning.

If the successful text inevitably sends its reader back to the world and restores him to the real, it is with a heightened awareness of his *total human responsibilities*, not simply a practical 'programme of action'. And this becomes possible only by virtue of the challenges and obstacles posed to the reader in his encounter with the text. The energy demanded of him fuses with the energy that constituted the text in the first place, to set free that complex new form of energy (mere electrical impulses now transformed into heat or light) which characterizes the assumption of responsibility to—and for— the world.

In different terms: the 'worthy' literary text invites the reader to the total involvement of a love-relationship: not a simple one-night stand, but the immersion of the self in the other in order that both may emerge from it more aware of their joint and several profundity and complexity. The text is a fully emancipated person, not a mindless little creature ready to fall back and open up. Her challenge is not the token resistance of the whore, but that of the integrated personality which yields neither to gentle persuasion nor to force but makes her own responsible decision about sharing only when the challenge from the other side is worthy of such commitment.

If the reader is invited to enter into an encounter with the text by those elements in it he can relate to because of their appearance of familiarity (man recognizing woman in terms of previous experience and of convention), the full relationship with it develops because of the challenge of the *un*familiar, the new, the strange, the defiance of *this* text which resists immediate consummation (the unknowable properties, the otherness of *this* person).

VI

I have spoken in sexual terms not only because it offered a comprehensive imagery which 'contains' my approach to literature as offence, but also because the sexual in itself represents an area of 'offensiveness' which seems to attract more persistent attention than many others. For every Dante who shocks his contemporaries for political, religious or other reasons, there are ten offenders in the moral sphere— an impression corroborated by most of the great literary *causes célèbres* of the past century: *Madame Bovary*, Zola, *Ulysses*, *Lady Chatterley's Lover*, *Lolita* . . .

It is an aspect of the subject which interests me because of the role sex has always played in my own work, and by the constant misrepresentation of it in South African (notably Afrikaans) criticism. And it is of importance to me because it has to do with what I am most deeply involved in: the experience and expression of human freedom, and the agony of human bondage.

Surely it is not just the processes and contortions of sex as such which account for the peculiar notion of offensiveness which colours the responses to it in countries incomparably more sophisticated than South Africa. (It is the persistence of such responses that make *Penthouse* and *Playboy* possible even in the blasé cultures and the open societies of the West.) The number of orifices and protuberances of the human body is finite; so is the range of their possible juxtapositions. If it had been no more than this—and if literature had *presented* it as no more than this—all vestiges of this ancient taboo would have disappeared totally, long ago.

In a sense, the reply is obvious and has been explored so often in recent years that it can be put in a nutshell. Sex, after all, *does* involve more than the union of poker and pokee. However many secondary or tertiary needs people may have been brainwashed into acquiring in our age of multiplicity, behind them all stand the three central 'facts', the three primary situations of the human condition which link individuals to humanity, to the natural world, and to their explorations of whatever lies beyond the 'merely' sensual, the 'merely' rational, the 'merely' biological: birth, sexual union and death. It is no coincidence, that, in religious practice, they are often enshrined as sacraments.

And of course they are intimately and intricately related: birth is the direct result of sex; the latter offers both affirmation of and a challenge to the death of the individual; death is in many religions held to imply a new beginning. No wonder that the fundamental relationship between God and humanity is so often described in sexual terms, ranging from The Song of Songs to St John of the Cross, from Tantric Buddhism to D. H. Lawrence.

In other words, there is indeed a profound motivation (practical, social, biological, religious, ethical, etc.) for the central position occupied by sex in human life; and so it is only logical that this should extend to the arts, if these are regarded as essential, and not peripheral, to life. It is one of the few 'universals' of existence, one of the few 'constants' persisting below the ebb and flood of customs, morals, cultures and fashions. Linking the individual to what is most primitive in himself, it remains one of the rare 'unknowns' of his experience, in spite of the great advances of learning and science. After examining every aspect of sexual behaviour which can conceivably be measured, catalogued or calculated, Masters and Johnson have not yet touched on the essence of *sex*—and assuredly not of love. And as long as it remains fundamentally unmappable, the urge to understand more about it will remain undiminished (and for just so long society's anxiety to protect it with taboos will persist). The moment somebody transgresses on this domain the community's defence mechanisms are alerted: what is primitive in the experience challenges sophistication; the hint of the unknown is potentially offensive.

There is another consideration. The moral sphere is one of the most crucial areas of contention in the struggle between generations, and in the tug of war between an authority and its subjects. Moral emancipation, because it is such an intensely personal process, is one of the primary signs of liberation in the individual—coinciding with, or facilitating, more public manifestations, including the political. And that, obviously, is something no regime can tolerate in a more or less unstable situation.

As long as the parent can preserve his child's sexual ignorance he retains his authority; or at least the illusion of his authority. From the onset of puberty parental authority is threatened until the position culminates in the final declaration of independence announced by the child's marriage. There is a parallel situation in politics. As long as an authority can persuade or force its subjects to accept that government is, in Brecht's words, 'a fate to be endured' rather

125

than a purely practical organization which can and may be changed or destroyed, it retains its power. And the adolescent who, in the era of the Pill, discovers that there is no absolute ethic governing pre-marital sex, but only a set of practical considerations, finds himself on the threshold of saying No to political absolutism as well.

In the light of this it is obvious that both the 'offence' and the reaction to it would be particularly violent when, in a literary work, the portrayal of sex should also acquire a political dimension. In South Africa, for example, a sexual relationship between black and white—because should this morality be accepted an entire political ideology will be threatened.

It involves a predictable pattern of cultural evolution which implies, among other things, that censorship is not only a sign of fear but of cultural immaturity; and as society or the individual advances and matures the need diminishes for this humiliating form of 'protection'—protection not so much against whatever the State defines as 'pornography' as against one's own reactions, and a deeper and more disturbing awareness of one's own self.

VII

The sexual serves as but one example of the way in which literature 'offends': the strategies of offence involve much more. A literature which does not constantly and insistently confront, affront, offend—and thereby explore and test and challenge—the reader and the world, is moribund.

If language is one of humanity's major instruments in its search for truth, its very nature demands of the writer never to cease from exploration—and to persist particularly when the offence it causes leads to a destructive system of counter-measures aimed at 'protecting' the weaknesses of the world. (In a society like South Africa the very threat of persecution

126

may suggest to the writer that he is heading in the right direction!)

Language is the marble of the writer: and in order to be worthy of it he should not flinch before whatever truth is exposed by his relentless chisel. Of course, he does not simply chip away marble in order to reveal some hidden form already there, enclosed in hardness. Galathea does not lie patiently inside, awaiting her birth, but is *brought into being* by the sculptor's dogged faith as much as by the cruel blows of his chisel. Once he has caused her to be born he has to live with her and accept full responsibility for her.

Part of the writer's responsibility to language, and to society which has provided him with it, lies in resisting every obstacle set up in the way of his exploration. However daunting may be the truth emerging from his work he has to learn to live with it, and to live up to it, rather than look for shelter behind the walls of taboo. The Unknown is there to be faced with the tools of the writer's trade. These tools do not strike into a vacuum but constantly encounter resistance which must be overcome. In the act of offence we glimpse the possibility of freedom.

As long as people can be offended by literature there remains a chance that they may be awakened from sleep in order to learn to face their world anew.

After Soweto

(1976)

Whom the gods wish to destroy . . . : this must have been a
spontaneous reflection in the minds of many as they saw the
eruption of violence in Soweto in June 1976, which spread
subsequently to engulf practically the whole of South Africa.
To most South Africa watchers abroad it came as no surprise;
yet it caught most white South Africans completely
unprepared. In the precarious lull which has followed the
storm (I am writing in the month of August) it may be
worthwhile to attempt a dispassionate, if necessarily brief,
'inside' evaluation of the situation as a whole: the gradual
emergence of apartheid, conceived initially as an experiment
in survival by a small group threatened from all sides, then
turning into a Frankenstein; the growing resistance to the
system within the country over the years; and the tensions
and relationships among the various population groups
today. Within this context I shall try to look at the options
open to the intellectual, notably to the (Afrikaans) writer
who, like myself, finds the system abhorrent and tries to fight
for liberty and justice in a society gone mad.

After Soweto

Random pictures from South African life today: Two well-dressed middle-aged black men are standing on a street corner, having a conversation. A police van draws up and an adolescent in uniform leans out. 'Hey, Kaffir!' he shouts. 'Come here. Show me your pass.' One of the black men produces his; the other has inadvertently left it at home when he changed his clothes this morning. He is grabbed and hurled into the back of the van where he may spend several hours before he is taken to the police station and locked up overnight until he can go to court the next morning and pay a fine. His next of kin are not informed. That he is a university lecturer makes no difference. He is black; he has to carry at all times the 'reference book' which is his sole claim to identity.

*

A coloured orchestra is invited to play at the wedding of a young white couple. They have to obtain special permission from the Department of Community Development. The permit is granted, but upon the condition that the coloured members of the orchestra are separated from the white guests by a fish-net curtain, in order to prevent 'mixing'.

*

A white South African marries a Vietnamese girl abroad. Then he is informed that should he bring his wife home with him, both of them can be jailed for 'immorality' because they do not belong to the same race. (If the girl were Japanese, an exception might be made; because Japan has enormous trade agreements with South Africa, consequently Japanese are regarded—for the duration of the contracts—as 'honorary whites'.)

129

*

An Indian doctor treats his white patient. But when the patient has to go to hospital, his doctor is no longer allowed to operate on him, because the operation theatre is for 'Whites Only'.

*

After a car accident two girls, one black, the other white, are left in a critical condition beside the road. An ambulance is called. But as it is for 'Whites Only' the black girl cannot be taken to hospital: she has to wait for a 'black' ambulance, even if the delay costs her her life.

*

Two newspaper editors, both highly respected men, are to be questioned by the Security Police on reports published in their respective papers. The white editor receives a phone call and is requested to come and see the police at 3 o'clock in the afternoon. The black editor is awakened at 4 o'clock in the morning by eight policemen who burst into his house, haul him away and keep him in detention until late afternoon before he is questioned and released.

*

A coloured man is found guilty of raping a white girl in a particularly brutal way and sentenced to death. In nearly similar circumstances a white man is found guilty of raping a black girl: after commenting on the atrocious nature of the crime the judge sentences the man to two years' imprisonment.

*

An Afrikaans farmer, respected and loved all his life by both the whites and coloureds of the small Western Cape community in which he lived, dies after a long illness. On the day of his funeral a number of coloured people also arrive for the church service, but they are turned away by the minister who will not allow them to pray together with whites.

Of course, one may conjure up other pictures as well: a white policeman risking his own life to save a black child from drowning. A black family, in the centre of the Soweto riots, sheltering a white journalist to save him from being stoned. An Afrikaans religious leader resigning from the white Dutch Reformed Church to become a member of a black congregation.

It is, indeed, 'a very strange society'.

II

A tendency towards separatism seems to be a legitimate political and moral impulse in minority societies—like those Irish who wish to separate themselves from the English, the Bretons who demand independence from France, the Basques who struggle so fiercely to be liberated from Spanish domination, the Quebecqois who insist on severing bonds with the rest of Canada. In these examples, however, there are some conditions radically different from the situation in South Africa. In the societies referred to minorities who feel their group identity threatened by a majority are striving for what they regard as liberation: it is the wish and demand of the people themselves. In South Africa an oppressed majority is being kept in bondage through the system of apartheid which guarantees white supremacy.

There is another consideration. If individuals or societies were to insist on separation on a basis of equality, of mutually

131

respected human dignity, there may be an undisputed moral legitimacy in their demands. This is not the case in South Africa.

Of course, apartheid has also been represented by its advocates as a moral way of solving the problems inherent in a multi-racial society, as an effort to eliminate friction between races at different stages of cultural development by allotting to each ethnic group its own geographical area where it can evolve to full political independence. And once such a constellation of independent 'homelands' is created, it is argued, mutual respect on a basis of national equality will follow, and discrimination based on colour will disappear. (It is the fallacy of all utopian thinking to justify the means in terms of the lofty end.)

However, the morality of the South African system becomes suspect the moment theory is measured against the all too harsh realities. First of all, as is only too well known, only 13 per cent of the land has been set aside for blacks, who number over 80 per cent of the population. Secondly, no separate 'homelands' are, or can be, provided for the 2.5 million coloureds (i.e. those people resulting from early miscegenation) and for the 800,000 Asiatics in the country. Although they are to have their own legislative and other institutions, they have no territory in which to exercise their functions. Even the black homelands are not homogeneous, unified territories: in some cases a 'homeland' consists of nine or more small patches of land spread all over the country, with white areas in between: a Gulag archipelago in a white ocean. And the millions of blacks who have become a permanent part of the population of 'white' cities are denied South African citizenship in favour of the practically fictitious citizenship of distant homelands where many of them have never set foot.

Above all, the flaw of apartheid lies in the fact that it is the construct of a handful of whites (4 million out of the country's population of some 25 million) and imposed on the vast majority of blacks without any attempt at significant consultation. As such, apartheid as a system is enforced from above and not, as the authorities would have it, one evolving naturally from South African history.

III

When the first Dutch colonists arrived at the Cape in 1652 it was with the intention of establishing a temporary halfway station only for the fleets of the Dutch East India Company, but within three years several of the settlers had decided to make it their permanent home and obtained their 'freedom' from the company in order to start farming on their own. In the course of the next century and a half a large portion of the interior was explored; and at a surprisingly early stage these farmers in the interior were thinking of themselves as 'Africans' as opposed to the 'European' officials at the Cape. It is important for an understanding of the Afrikaner today to realize that, for more than three centuries, he has regarded himself as a 'native' of Africa: there is a radical difference between his position and that of, say, the English in India, or the French in Algeria.

And this situation was reinforced by the fact that, at the time the first Dutch arrived, most of the Cape country appeared to be practically uninhabited. The only people encountered by the early colonists were nomadic tribes of the Khoisan peoples ('Bushmen' and 'Hottentots') who appeared to have no fixed territory and roamed throughout the interior. In other words there was, at that stage, no 'annexation' of land belonging to others: the land appeared to be available for the taking (even though much of this may have been based on misunderstanding). At a very early stage, too, the Khoisan peoples were decimated by epidemics of smallpox; many of the Sān ('Bushmen') retreated to other parts of the country; a number of the remaining Khoin

('Hottentots') were incorporated into 'white' society through miscegenation.

It must be emphasized that racialistic feelings as such were almost non-existent at that early stage. Although there were few marriages between black and white, there was little shame attached to such unions (and what shame there was seemed to be based on social, not racial, considerations); the numerous offspring of liaisons between white masters and Malay or other slaves or free Hottentots formed the nucleus of the increasing 'coloured' population of today. From a very early stage they adopted the Dutch language; and by the time this language had evolved into what is today known as Afrikaans, most coloureds were Afrikaans-speaking. (In fact, in the late nineteenth century, when many Afrikaners were ashamed of speaking their own language, which was then regarded as a patois, and preferred English which had become the language of high society, the coloureds kept alive the Afrikaans language, nourished it and contributed immeasurably to its final survival and triumph.)

If a sense of racial superiority was experienced in the first century or so of Cape history, it was based on social and religious considerations and, notably, on the practice of slavery. The whites regarded themselves as being sent to the 'Dark Continent' by God in order to save it from ignorance and heathen practices. It was, of course, an attitude prevalent all over the world at the time. But gradually, in most of the rest of the world, a moment arrived when a definite choice had to be made to incorporate 'others' into the existing societies, and to incur the effort and expense involved in educating and 'elevating' the more or less 'barbaric' masses. This decision was deferred in South Africa for more than two centuries, until 'Christianity' and 'civilization' appeared to become identified with 'whiteness'. Much of this, as I shall try to point out, was inspired by economic considerations.

Towards the end of the eighteenth century two decisive

confrontations took place in South Africa: the first encounter with the black Bantu-speaking races driving southward, and the first annexation of the colony by Britain. It is indicative of the 'African-ness' of the Dutch farmers in the interior that their first reaction to British takeover was an—abortive—effort to establish two small independent republics in the interior. It is of great significance, too, that on several occasions in the course of the nineteenth century there were attempts by Afrikaners and black Africans to join forces against British imperialism.

The history of confrontation with the black tribes is essentially one of tragic misunderstanding. Both sides felt they had 'right' on their side; neither understood the territorial claims of the other. They regularly met as enemies, yet both believed that they belonged essentially to Africa. (Would the confrontation have had different results if the Boers had not been conditioned, in their relations with blacks, by the long experience of slavery?) Both had an essentially peasant attachment to the soil, a fierce sense of tribal identity, an almost mystical communion with the land.

The presence of the British colonizers changed the course of history. From the Second British Occupation (from 1806 onwards) a separation of the races was attempted, essentially in order to avoid conflict. They brought with them the strangely ambivalent attitude of the Christian colonizer: believing in the primal innocence of the 'noble savage'—yet continuing to treat him in situations of personal contact as an inferior, a 'native'. The gravitational centre of the British colonizer remained London. That was the seat of civilization and supremacy; everything else was inferior. And so, although the British effected the emancipation of the slaves and endless measures aimed at improving the lot of the blacks, they did it so clumsily, with such an aloof attitude of having all right on their side, that relations between the races in the country were permanently scarred. In the brown and black races of Southern Africa British philanthropists kindled new hopes and ideals—promptly thwarted by the practical machinations of British imperialism which resorted mainly to power politics in order to plough all obstacles into the ground (followed by lofty moral justifications of all such acts). At the same time the Afrikaners were made the scapegoat of every racial confrontation on the frontiers; and although many wrongs were undoubtedly righted or prevented by British intervention, they also created in the minds of Afrikaners a deep-rooted conviction of being persecuted, misunderstood, insulted and generally treated unjustly. A certain masochism may even have emerged from the experience: the conviction of having right on one's side *because* of the hostility and prejudice one experienced. The very harshness of the imperialist ruler became proof of one's own moral rectitude. And rather than bow to injustice the tribe was prepared to trek into the wilderness and follow the example of Moses and his people, in search of a new Promised Land. The religious fervour with which Afrikanerdom relived, in the Great Trek and its aftermath, the history of the Old Testament, influenced decisively their attitude towards the blacks scattered throughout the interior in the great *difaqane* caused by Chaka: these were now the new hostile and heathen tribes of Canaan who had to be conquered in the name of the Lord . . .

Wherever the migrants went—to the Orange Free State, to Natal, to the Transvaal—their new territories were eventually re-annexed by Britain. As a result, another significant trait of the Afrikaner character was reinforced in these years: whenever he landed in trouble and felt threatened, he packed his wagons and moved away. When cornered by an enemy he pulled his wagons into a circle, a *laager*, from which he fought. On the one hand, this imbued in him a sense of evasion or postponement of problems: rather than solve something, it was easier to move off. On the other hand, it created a feeling of being threatened and beleaguered from all sides, with the only safety to be found inside the *laager* of his own people.

Essentially, I believe, one can evaluate the Trek and its subsequent history, as a search for identity on the part of the Afrikaner: a small nation that had come into being in a strange and hostile land and which had managed to survive only by drawing on the resources of Africa.

For a brief period there was 'peace' in the interior, after the founding of two Boer Republics. But the discovery of diamonds and gold rekindled an old mercenary and colonialist instinct in the British, who soon found pretexts for ignominiously repossessing the Republics. And unfortunately malpractices in those Republics, notably in Paul Kruger's Transvaal, made it possible for Britain to find the pretexts she needed. After a bloody war, which still to an alarming extent determines relations between Afrikaners and English in South Africa today, the Free State and Transvaal became British possessions again in 1902, followed by a period of deliberate anglicizing through education and other means. Once again Afrikaner identity was at stake; once again the people had to fight for physical survival.

In this continued struggle race again played its part. It was impossible to defeat the English; and so frustrations were vented by avenging it on the blacks. (For obvious reasons many blacks had joined the British forces against the Boers in the war.)

IV

After the four colonies were united in the Union of 1910, two strong nationalist movements simultaneously announced themselves: an Afrikaner movement in the National Party; and a black movement in the African National Congress. The National Party finally gained power by winning the elections in 1948. The ANC, because blacks were not entitled to vote, had no hope of winning constitutionally and so eventually had to resort to other means. But essentially the struggle of both movements ran parallel to one another.

The situation was compounded by economic problems, notably the rise of industrialism and capitalism. The Afrikaners, hitherto an essentially rural people, were drawn from their farms to the big cities and the mines where, soon, a large white proletariat was formed. And inspired by the Russian Revolution of 1917 Afrikaner workers attempted to beat the big mine bosses by striking. That was the time when one of their leaders, later to become prime minister, Dr D. F.Malan, openly extolled the virtues of Socialism.

But it was a curious form of Socialism, since it was essentially white-oriented. The violence on the mines in the early 1920s was directed as much against the English capitalist bosses as against the threat of black workers who, willing to accept lower wages, threatened the livelihood of the white proletariat. A century earlier the threat of the blacks was physical and military; now, on the economic and social front, the threat had become more subtle and hence more dangerous. The Afrikaner, threatened both from 'above' and 'below', realized that his very survival as a group with its own identity was at stake.

For a long time the coloureds were not really felt to be a threat. Culturally and linguistically they were Afrikaners; they were largely confined to the Cape where industrialization was slow to be introduced, and so the Afrikaner did not really fear them so much. The Indians lived mainly in Natal, where they had been imported to work on English sugar estates: they, too, were no threat to the Afrikaner. (In the case both of coloureds and of Indians, of course, the numerical factor is decisive: to white they represent a minority, unlike the masses of the black majority.) Even in the 1930s Dr Malan promised eventual integration with the coloureds.

But by the time the National Party won the elections in 1948 industrialization had increased; moreover, it appeared that many coloureds preferred to vote for Jan Smuts's Opposition party which was more British-oriented. And so the coloureds, who until that time had had full voting rights in the Cape, had to be deprived of the vote by the very man who had once promised them full participation, Dr Malan. This process now developed further and further until today the hostility between coloureds and whites has reached alarming proportions; in addition, many coloureds are said to turn to English, renouncing their mother tongue, Afrikaans.

At the time when the Afrikaner assumed political control (1948), the whole economic structure of the country was still dominated by English; even today most of the economy is still in English hands. In addition, for a long time after 1948, South African culture remained predominantly English. Which means that, even though he had taken over the political power, the Afrikaner continued to feel threatened. Once again the '*laager* mentality' came to the fore, asserting itself in the sad saga of repressive legislation which has come to characterize the regime. Previously, racial intermarriage was frowned upon socially, but it was not illegal. Now all sexual intercourse between races became illegal—in a belated and ridiculous effort to 'purify' the race. Buses and beaches and trains had been integrated before 1948; now the races were no longer free to travel or swim or go to the theatre or have sport together. And only very recently (because of the effective isolation of South Africa in the sports world, not from any moral consideration) have attempts been made to reverse this process.

Verwoerd, the great theoretician, introduced his grand concept of splitting up the entire country on the basis of ethnic grouping: every individual had to be 'classified'—with the most absurd consequences. Contact between races had to be minimized if not altogether eliminated. Even university education had to become segregated, with an alarming drop in academic standards. (The 'black' universities, where libraries are under strict control and students constantly surveilled by Security Police, and where academic qualifications are often secondary to political convictions, are generally referred to as 'Bush Colleges'.) Primary and secondary education for blacks is of a shocking standard, being designed specifically to prepare blacks for a situation of social inferiority and exploitability. In addition, it is expensive, which means that relatively few blacks can afford it. (White education, ironically enough, is free.) For years ideology determined everything in the country, from politics to the most private relationships; the Great Ideal deliberately obscured the realities of everyday life. From now on, a person's place of abode is determined by his colour, as is the nature of his work and the limits of his progress within it. The entire South African capitalist economy depends on the cheap labour of blacks 'imported' from the homelands or neighbouring countries. These migrant workers are housed in vast dormitories where only males are allowed, while their families remain in the homelands. Not only does this cause a terrible disruption of family and social life, but the sexual tensions which build up, aggravated by the presence of large groups of hostile tribesmen in confined quarters, often lead to explosions.

In reality, *everybody* falls victim to the system. A small, pathetic example: in 1902 an Italian man came to South Africa, married a black woman and settled in the Johannesburg suburb of Sophiatown. In the early 1950s, after the death of his wife, he lived with his daughter; but as Sophiatown was now declared 'white only' (depriving the many blacks who still possessed houses and land there of their freehold rights), his daughter had to move. They went to another 'mixed' suburb. But a few years later this area was declared 'coloured' and the old man, then totally blind and more than eighty years old, was not allowed to continue living with his own daughter (who was, of course, 'coloured'). He died destitute. Multiply this kind of suffering by thousands and something of the essential inhumanity of the South African scene becomes evident.

No wonder that some reaction had to set in, culminating

finally in the 1976 violence in Soweto and elsewhere, leaving in its wake hundreds of dead, thousands of arrested, and damages running into millions. It would seem that a new act in the drama of the South African Revolution has begun.

V

But the conflagrations of Soweto must be seen against the background of a dedicated resistance against apartheid which had been building up for years. Within the white group, English speakers had initially tried to organize resistance to Afrikaner political power at the polls, but lost heart when the National Party increased its majority with every election during the 1950s—at first through shrewd re-delimitation of constituencies, later through the sheer momentum acquired by white Nationalism itself (both as a positive force through which long-suppressed Afrikaner aspirations could be satisfied, and as a negative, i.e. anti-black, force stimulated by fear). From then onwards English resistance was mainly effected in the domain of economics, but when even that form of pressure was successfully countered, a large portion of the English population simply seemed to lapse into apathy: if they could not control political power they would rather have nothing to do with it at all. Since the late 1960s a strong rebirth of political feeling became manifest at English universities. Acting from purely moral considerations, in order to express solidarity with the oppressed and voiceless black majority, these English students introduced new momentum into South African political life—but through brutal suppression, matching police action elsewhere in the world, this movement was short-lived and at present a feeling of impotent malaise seems to predominate in English university circles.

For some time white critics of apartheid continued to fight the dangerous new order of legalized and systematized discrimination by siding with blacks in the only multi-racial political party in the country, the Communist Party (which included numerous non-communist members who co-operated simply because that was the only forum in which political opposition could be effectively organized). After the Communist Party was outlawed, the novelist Alan Paton's Liberal Party carried on the struggle for a just and Christian multi-racial society—until, in the late 1960s, that too was disbanded when a new Act of Parliament prohibited multi-racial membership of political parties.

In the meantime the different black organizations—the ANC, the Indian Congress (founded years before by Mahatma Gandhi) and the Coloured People's Organization—continued their struggle against the never-ending process of further eroding their precarious liberties. Through all the years (including the Second World War years when extremist Afrikaner Nationalists conducted a campaign of sabotage against the Government's support of Britain) these movements remained strictly within the law in carrying on their non-violent struggle. Even when their very existence became threatened by the triumph of the National Party in 1948 their resistance remained peaceful—though its operations intensified in a campaign of peaceful defiance of discriminatory laws. The only result was more intimidation and persecution: in 1952 some 8,500 men, women and youths were imprisoned because they had *peacefully* disobeyed the latest dehumanizing laws of the apartheid system. The leaders were convicted under the new Suppression of Communism Act (even though few of them actually were communists; in fact, several were strongly anti-communist). The 1950s became a decade of strikes aimed at emphasizing the grievances of the voiceless. Even these strikes were illegal, but the movement persisted because it was a form of protest both non-violent and spectacular. In June 1950 the police retaliated by killing eighteen people in one day, which was but one of many similar incidents.

142

The resistance movement also assumed another form, mainly through the massive meeting of June 1955, where 2,000 delegates from all races met near Johannesburg to adopt, in spite of vicious police intimidation, a 'Freedom Charter' for the future development of the country. Not only was this ignored by the Government, but more than 156 of the leaders of this movement were arrested on charges of high treason. The absurdity of the move was demonstrated when, after a mammoth trial lasting five years, all the accused were found innocent.

Soon afterwards a terrible climax was reached with the killing of more than sixty peaceful demonstrators by police in the now historic massacre of Sharpeville in March 1960, followed by widespread unrest throughout the country— resulting in the arrest of more than 10,000 people and the imprisonment of more than 2,000 leading black figures.

This prompted a new style of tactics based on sabotage and underground propaganda. Still the emphasis remained on non-personal violence. And once again, in March 1961, the African leaders of the country made a peaceful call on the Government to convene a National Convention in order to work out a common future for all the inhabitants of the country. Once again the response was violent: new draconian laws empowering detention without trial, new raids, new jailings. And the 1960s became characterized by a near-endless series of political trials, the most famous being the 'Rivonia Trial' which resulted in the life imprisonment of great black leaders like Nelson Mandela and Walter Sisulu; and the trial of the famous Afrikaner resistance leader Bram Fischer, on charges of planning sabotage and 'furthering the aims of communism'. Although he had clearly devised his whole strategy in such a way as to avoid danger to human life, the facts were represented in such a way as to brand him a 'terrorist' and he, too, was sent to jail for life. (When he contracted cancer ten years later, he was finally allowed out on parole to die in the house of his brother; but after the

143

funeral the government claimed his ashes. For even the ashes of a free man can be dangerous in a state ruled by fear and suspicion.)

And so it seemed that the only result of peaceful resistance was even less liberty and more suppression than before. Moreover, a new post-Sharpeville generation of blacks was growing up, who blamed their own parents for their present degradation, and accused them of condoning the system by not opposing it more forcefully.

In the meantime, the Government's homeland policy had advanced considerably, creating new black 'leaders' (carefully selected on the principle of His Master's Voice) to work within the system of apartheid. Some played the game; in more than one case, it seems, the possibility of gaining immense personal power and wealth through co-operating with the Government, acted as a strong incentive. (And some proved to be good disciples. Even before Transkei became 'independent' in 1976, most of the effective opposition in that territory was in jail!) Others, like the Zulu leader, Gatsha Buthelezi, skilfully manipulated the situation to challenge the Government at their own game: realizing that open resistance could only lead to more loss of freedom, they used the very framework of apartheid to foster black aspirations. Coinciding with an inevitable rise of Black Consciousness (the exact counterpart of the earlier awakening of the Afrikaner's aggressive discovery of identity) this became a factor of considerable weight on the South African scene.

VI

And yet, in spite of all the increasing signs of oppression, a more positive direction was beginning to assert itself below the surface (partly, too, as a result of the action of leaders like Buthelezi created by apartheid but turning the tables on their masters). The *true face* of South Africa was beginning to look

144

different from the intolerant and intolerable mask of apartheid. Fostered by the increasing economic affluence of the country which had also begun to affect blacks (in however limited a way), increasing 'internationalization' through communications with the rest of the world, and increasing educational standards among blacks, a natural evolutionary process began to emerge.

After all, South Africa was trying to impose an imperialistic/capitalistic system precisely at a time when the rest of the world was beginning to move away from it. And even though, on the surface, the country continued to reject criticism from outside, its economic situation and its growing exposure to the international world was beginning to open up more possibilities for natural evolution than before.

A point of possible change was reached with the announcement of South Africa's policy of 'detente' in Africa—culminating in the historic meeting between Prime Minister Vorster and President Kaunda of Zambia in 1975; and at the same time the South African Ambassador in the USA announced that the country would do all it could 'to move away from discrimination'.

Today, a mere eighteen months later, South Africa is, more than ever before, a stench in the nostrils of the world. And Vorster, once hailed as the 'peacemaker' in Africa, has become not only a symbol of disillusionment and despair but, in fact, the major obstacle to significant change in South Africa. From the stature of a statesman he has dwindled into a bewildered political animal dominated by fear and the basic instinct of survival.

What has brought about this change?

VII

In the first place, Vorster initiated a movement of foreign detente without linking it to significant *internal* change.

In a famous BBC interview Alexander Solzhenitsyn warned the West against detente: Russia, he said, was offering one hand to the West while keeping the other concealed behind its back. That was exactly Vorster's clumsy manoeuvre in an effort to gain all the possible advantage of neutralizing African countries through cordial trade and other ties while refusing to normalize the intolerable position in his own country.

The death-blow to significant detente was, of course, caused by South Africa's disastrous involvement in the Angolan war. That this adventure may have been based on an 'understanding' that the USA would also intervene, is no excuse. All it reveals is a staggering inability to grasp the simplest realities of the situation: anyone expecting the US to get involved in a foreign adventure so soon after Vietnam, and in an election year to boot, should have had his mind read. And so the South African troops (whose very presence in Angola was denied by the Government while they were within striking distance of Luanda) had to turn back. They may have won every battle on their way, as the South African Minister of Defence so frantically insisted, yet they have lost the war as surely as Britain eventually lost the Anglo-Boer War. And suddenly, so soon after the establishment of a Marxist regime in Mozambique, South Africa saw the liberation of another black state on its borders.

For the first time since their long peaceful struggle began, blacks in South Africa realized that emancipation was no longer a dream but a strong probability. (Unfortunately the situation is complicated immeasurably by the presence of Russian and Cuban military power in Angola: a natural process of change in South Africa may be inhibited by the fear that 'the Russians are coming'—which may, in the minds of many, lead to worse repression than before. A significant number of whites who would actively promote change are now held back for fear of another Hungary or Czechoslovakia. And many blacks in South Africa, too, may

146

dread the simplistic exchange of one form of suppression for another. Solzhenitsyn's voice is only too loud in one's ears.)

In these circumstances the Black Month of June 1976 dawned in South Africa. Angered by the 'inertia' of their parents, inspired by the possibility of real success, frustrated—among many other things—by an education system forcing them to learn many subjects through the medium of a third language, Afrikaans (which had already, to them, become 'the language of the oppressor'), and finally considering that, live or die, they really had nothing to lose, the youth of the sprawling black conglomeration of Soweto (denied even the dignity of being called a 'city', since the inhabitants are only 'tolerated' by whites and their very existence as citizens is denied) went into action. Violence erupted all over the country. At the moment, as a result of unprecedented police action, an uneasy calm has descended. But already it is evident that 'Soweto' represents not just a moment of transition like Sharpeville: it is an effective watershed. Life in South Africa will never again be the same.

The only relevant question is: will the dénouement of this final act be peaceful or violent by nature? And I must make it absolutely clear: a *peaceful solution* implies the acceptance of all the implications of living in a permanently multi-racial society; a *violent solution* may aim at the elimination of the white presence as a political factor from the South African scene—because in a war of this nature not all the formidable military and economic power of white South Africa can win in the long run.

VIII

If one can still contemplate a peaceful transition—in which case, more than ever before, time is the decisive element— the position and role of the Afrikaner is of vital importance.

At this moment he is in power; it lies in his hands to introduce effective change. Yet in the two months since the first explosion in Soweto the authorities have given little sign of a readiness to change—*little sign, in fact, of even appreciating the extent of what is at stake.* In the same week that Soweto erupted, for example, the Government rejected most of the really significant recommendations of the Theron Report on the situation and future of the coloureds. (Since then there has been a marked deterioration in white–coloured relationships and a more overt identification of coloureds with the *black* cause.) In other words: even in a week of total crisis the Government went ahead with discriminatory practices and projections in a way which can only be termed apocalyptic arrogance. A Freudian death-wish, the Afrikaner's Masada complex, should never be underestimated. If die he must, he will do so with a bang, not a whimper.

And yet, among many Afrikaners—not those belonging to the small clique who rule the country (*après nous le déluge*)— there is a remarkable readiness today to implement drastic change. Obviously this is evident mainly among intellectuals, who can 'afford' to feel safe. But it is manifesting itself as widening soul-searching in many circles. If it *really* becomes a matter of survival, I believe Afrikaners will be prepared to adapt. They have survived for 300 years because, even though they often fled rather than fought, they have learnt to contend with African realities.

For many years there has been a small band of intrepid Afrikaner intellectuals (among them the greatly respected Beyers Naudé, who heads the Christian Institute) who left the safety of the *laager* to plead for justice on a wider scale: an awareness of a country's obligations to the twentieth century. In recent years a few Afrikaans writers have joined this group. And, significantly, since the Soweto violence a number of Afrikaans newspaper editors have also become more outspoken in their demands for change.

There has always been a curious schism between private

and public opinion among Afrikaners. I have often come across men, even in high government positions, with extremely liberal views when they find themselves among friends: but the moment they appear in public, all the old conservative clichés reappear. Now at last the general reaction to Soweto and the outspoken views of newspapers may contribute to the discovery that dissatisfaction among Afrikaners themselves is not limited to isolated individuals any longer, but is amazingly widespread. From this discovery the previously pusillanimous may draw the courage required to speak their minds more openly. And in this I find at least a small glimmer of hope.

IX

What would peaceful change involve? To begin with, surely, the assembly of a convention representative of all people in the country (similar to that in progress in Namibia, where after many years a prospect of such a peaceful changeover is, in fact, emerging) to decide on our common future. This would inevitably entail the dismantling of the entire apartheid structure inasmuch as it is based on the exploitation of inequality. It may well be that certain groups (like the Xhosas who have now become 'independent' in their 'own' Transkei) may insist on some form of ethnic grouping, which could most easily be accommodated in a federal system. *But the entire framework of discrimination will have to be abolished.*

Much of the future lies in the hands of the South African blacks themselves. That, to me, is the really decisive change brought about by Soweto. The initiative is no longer solely the prerogative of whites. *It no longer depends upon what whites are prepared to give, but on what blacks are prepared to accept or to allow.* Blacks realize to what an extent the South African economy depends on them: in spite of all repressive measures they cannot be coerced into being exploited any more. They can at last begin to dictate their own terms. The dismantling has, in fact, begun—even though not much of it may be readily visible on the surface yet.

X

What is the function, the possibilities, of a writer living under this rumbling volcano?

There are countries in which the social or political climate makes it relatively easy for a writer to withdraw into an ivory tower and grapple with metaphysical problems. There are others, and South Africa is such a one, in which the socio-political realities are so overwhelming that no escape is possible. In fact, the difficult situation arises where one's involvement with the anguish of others consumes so much of one's creative energies that little may remain to devote to writing. But in this moment of terrible choice between peace and violence, I as a writer must try to define my position, knowing only too well that, especially in the last decade, the world has come to view with great suspicion the role of the intellectual in general. Yet much depends not only on one's view of the intellectual but on the nature of that intellectual himself, and on the nature of the society in which he operates.

It is true that 'the Liberal' is regarded with suspicion, if not open hostility, in the world—and often justly so, if his role amounts to escapism and mere 'moral support'. And in a society like the South African, where blacks have to experience all the brutalities of the system while white Liberals can never be more than mere hangers-on (some with a view towards saving themselves in a holocaust), blacks have every right to reject liberalism. They have had enough of sanctimonious meddling, charity, and good causes. They cannot bear it any more. And so they prefer to go it alone.

But that does not absolve any white from getting involved

in the situation. There are certain prerogatives which have justly passed into the hands of blacks; but surely there remain enormous responsibilities to be assumed by whites as well— *even if they may well be obliterated as individuals by what lies ahead.* As a white man I have an historical responsibility towards this particular moment in history.

The writer may often despair about his inability to do more than to think or to write. Since the age of the Romantics writers have experienced what one critic termed 'the fatal lure of action'. 'What is the good of having been the first poet of one's country,' asked Lamartine in words which might just as well have been uttered by Breyten Breytenbach, 'if one does not become its first man of action?' It is indeed the tragedy of the intellectual, as Emmanuel Berl pointed out, that he would like to be a revolutionary but cannot make it. And yet this argument is essentially warped, as it arises from the old and unnecessary dichotomy between 'words' and 'acts'. Within the context of a situation like the one in South Africa writing can, and does, become effective as a revolutionary act in its own, peculiar, right.

It seems to me that the Afrikaans writer has a special responsibility in this context. Because of the very nature of his situation—the fact that, through history, culture and the colour of his skin he is linked, like it or not, to the power Establishment, nothing he says or writes takes place in a vacuum: it always elicits a *response*. The authorities, sensitive about being 'stabbed in the back' by 'one of our own', react— and overreact—in such a way as to sensationalize the event. A younger generation of Afrikaners reacts with a surge of enthusiasm, challenging in the process the monolith of power. Even more important: a book written by an Afrikaner dissident draws significant echoes from the silent world of the oppressed. The deepest joy I have known as a writer has been on the occasions when black or coloured compatriots, some of whom have not even read my work, have written or spoken to me to tell me of a new ray of hope in their lives.

In such a situation the writer has two important responsibilities. The first is, quite simply, to keep the people informed. In a country dominated by official lies and distortions and, alarmingly, by an increasing silence among well-meaning people who have lost their curiosity and who have allowed themselves to be coaxed or bludgeoned into accepting without question whatever happens, a growing number of whites simply *do not know*—and do not *want* to know—what is happening. Soweto has shocked most of them out of their complacency. But the human mind is remarkably effective in blocking out what is unpleasant or intolerable. And the writer, among others, can ensure that the terrible excuse of Nuremberg is not heard again.

The writer's second responsibility, much more important than the first (for the first hardly goes beyond the level of journalism, however important that in itself may be) is to explore and expose the roots of the *human condition* as it is lived in South Africa: a grappling with essentials, with the fundamentals of human experience and human relationships, *sup specie historiae*. By keeping alive the voice of reason and the search for meaning in a demented world he offers a safeguard to human dignity and an awareness of human values. If the writer falls silent, it becomes that much easier for society to sink back into the swamp of violence and hysteria. For violence is essentially and inevitably a denial of human dignity: and so it seems to me that the act of writing is profoundly anti-violent. Even—and especially—in a situation where violence cannot be avoided, it is imperative for the voice of the writer to be heard.

Writing, in this sense, far from being an evasion of responsibility, becomes an involvement with the human situation at its deepest level.

This in itself, in a country like South Africa, is a hazardous occupation: with every word he utters the writer places himself at stake, which is the only test for the full assumption of responsibility.

There can be no doubt about the fact that the black writer is more exposed to the full weight of repressive measures than any white writer can ever be. Yet one should not underestimate the hazards threatening the white writer: and a very special form of persecution is reserved for the Afrikaans writer who is regarded by the political establishment as a traitor to the cause. The Security Police is ever alert to suppress or inhibit the truth. Often the persecution is brutal and overt. More often it is subtle and destructive on a less exposed level. I have enough personal experience of this by now to know my enemy. From this knowledge I derive the urgent conviction that, while there is still time, in this turbulent silence preceding the final storm, the writer has no choice but to expose and proclaim the truth wherever he can and wheresoever he perceives it. If he is no longer allowed to shout, he must learn to speak in another tone of voice. If that is denied him, he must begin to whisper. And if he is no longer allowed even to whisper he must, in Artaud's memorable phrase, continue to signal through the flames.

Of Slaves and Masters

(1978)

For a long time it has been a widely held view that black-white relations in South Africa, originating from contact between free nations, have no true parallel in countries like the US where such relations were conditioned by the initial inequality between master and slave. But in the course of my research for a new novel I have been working on for some time, it has become more and more clear to me that attitudes prevalent in a community like the one at the Cape in the early nineteenth century can shed some disquieting light on the situation today.

To start with some general reflections, there exists an intriguing similarity between certain patterns of change in South Africa in recent years and the tortuous movement towards the abolition of slavery in 1834.

In a society based on inequality and exploitation, early nineteenth-century colonists often quite sincerely thought that they were doing as much as could be expected of any decent Christian if they taught their slaves to sing hymns and learn by heart passages from the Gospel (which, of course, condoned slavery) and if they treated them 'well'—which meant not overworking them, not flogging them more than was thought necessary (say thirty-nine stripes for mild neglect of duty), not selling members of a family separately before the children had reached a certain age, providing them with a reasonable quantity of food and some form of shelter.

After all, a slave cost a lot of money and in order to expect a fair yield on his investment it was in the owner's interest to keep his slaves as comfortable as possible so that they could work for as long as possible.

Many Cape slaves were allowed to set up shops or become artisans in their own right, prospering on a small scale within the noble framework or more or less free enterprise. They were often allowed substantial freedom of movement, provided they carried a pass signed by the master. Many slave women were the acknowledged concubines of their owners, and more often than not white children were brought up by slaves.

The problem started when the possibility of emancipation was first suggested by people like Wilberforce. (Interesting to note that to this day certain English farmers in the Eastern Cape refer to blacks as 'Wilbies'.)

For more than twenty years after 1807, when the slave trade was abolished, the British Government, wishing to avoid any confrontation with the colonial slave owners on whom so much of the empire's wealth depended, continued to play a precarious game of 'reasonable reforms'.

Instead of eradicating the evil itself by abolishing slavery as such, a long series of attempts were aimed at making the best of a bad business.

In 1816, for example, a proclamation enforced the registration of all Cape slaves, and in 1823 the lot of slaves was further alleviated by limiting working hours, restricting punishment, facilitating slave marriages and so on.

Three years later 'slave protectors' were introduced and in 1830 owners were instructed to keep a record of punishment inflicted.

All these efforts, enforced from abroad, still acknowledged the system of slavery and merely attempted to alleviate some of the hardships inherent in the system. And only in December 1834 was slavery itself abolished.

The irony, of course, was that, without these measures and the interference of the British Government, slavery at the Cape might have been abolished long before that date. Even before the second British occupation of the Cape in 1806 the Batavian rulers had proposed the emancipation of all girl slaves at birth, which would have eradicated slavery in a 'natural' way within a single generation.

And in the course of the following decades the Cape slave owners themselves repeatedly made similar or slightly modified proposals for abolition—but the British Government, hampered no doubt by the consideration of treating all colonies equally, refused to comply.

The protests at the Cape against measures controlling slavery involved some ludicrous impracticalities of the regulations enforced by Britain, not the notion of abolition as such. And the outcry against abolition when it finally came had little to do with the fact of the emancipation of slaves, and concerned mainly the bungling manner in which it was effected (the abruptness of the move, inadequate compensation, and so on).

The result was a decisive split between British (i.e. foreign) rulers and Afrikaner colonists, as the procedures of emancipation became a major cause of the Great Trek of Boers into the interior.

There is no simple parallel between slave emancipation and the present situation in a beleaguered South Africa. For one thing, in the nineteenth century the more significant changes towards liberation were proposed from inside the country, the cosmetic changes from abroad—today it is largely the other way round.

Also, it may be disputable whether today the Afrikaner would really be prepared to introduce fundamental changes if the 'outside world' stopped goading him (often, unfortunately, with highly suspect motives and a rather selective morality).

Yet I suspect that the Afrikaner would accept radical change if he could be persuaded from the inside (by his own leaders, as he is still, however anachronistically, strongly leader-oriented) that such a change would be a condition for his own survival.

In the most recent past events in Namibia have pointed in this direction, which highlights the failure of the existing South African Government to convince the electorate of the basic imperatives of the situation.

One is more and more tempted to think that, for the South African authorities, it is no longer even the survival of whites that takes precedence, but quite simply the retention of their personal power for as long as they can still hold on—and *après eux le déluge*. Which is why it resembles a scorched earth policy.

Against this broad general background more specific issues can be explored.

In the wake of the eruption of Soweto and the vicious repressive measures of October 1976, the only two instances of more or less organized slave revolts in Cape history appear especially significant.

The first, larger in scope if less dramatic in content, involved some 330 slaves who started a revolt in the Koeberg, Tygerberg and Swartland regions in 1808. Inspired by what, today, would be termed two foreign 'agitators' (one of them Irish!), the leaders rounded up the slaves on thirty-four farms, tied up the masters, drank up their brandy, and marched on Cape Town where they arrived in a state of total inebriety.

Needless to say, the rebellion was quashed and the leaders were punished, several of them with the death penalty. (Most of the followers, allegedly recruited without really knowing what was going on, were sent home—presumably to private punishment by their masters.)

What concerns us in the present context is that the uprising was motivated by the announcement, in 1807, of the abolition of the slave trade. The rebellious slaves, under the impression that slavery as such was to be abolished, were shattered when the expected liberty did not materialize— hence the resort to arms, an act unthinkable during the preceding 150 years of Cape history when slavery had appeared to be an immutable condition.

Of much more relevance to us is the second revolt, which occurred in the remote Bokkeveld region of the Worcester district in February 1825. Twelve slaves and one free man (the latter was soon discharged) were accused of murdering three white men and wounding a white woman, in an attempt to free themselves and inspire others to follow their example, with the ultimate aim of taking over the colony.

Following a rumour about new measures in connection with slavery to be promulgated in the near future, they were somehow led to believe that it would involve their emancipation. In addition, some of them had overheard their masters discussing the unbearable restrictions imposed on owners and expressing the resolve rather to shoot all their slaves than set them free.

The date of Christmas 1824 or New Year's Day 1825 was mentioned as the Day of Liberation. When that day came and went without any sign of freedom the young slave Galant, as previously arranged with his family and comrades, killed the master with whom he had grown up as a child and the brief and violent revolt was under way.

In court it was emphasized that Galant and the others had not been motivated by revenge. True, all of them had suffered, in one way or another, terrible punishment at the hands of their owners. Galant himself had on several occasions been flogged, often on several consecutive days. One woman had once been tied up and thrown into a river, nearly drowning before she was hauled out again. In addition to being subjected to several monstrous beatings, she had often been forced to walk about naked in winter.

Galant's one-year-old child had allegedly been beaten to

death with a *sjambok* because he had crawled after his mother and disturbed her in her duties.

But not one of the accused really complained about this treatment. The tenor of their testimony was that, as slaves, they expected and accepted punishment. It was part of their daily existence and they did not question their master's right to use or abuse them as he wished.

But what did spark off the revolt, what finally compelled a 'favourite' slave to kill the man who had been his closest childhood companion, was that rumour of a freedom which never materialized. They were prepared to suffer torture. But they refused to submit to the cruelty of hopes raised and not fulfilled. (Grist to the mill of the modern reactionary: 'I told you so, didn't I? Offer these people your little finger and they grab your arm. Only way to manage them is to keep them down. You start toying with reform and you end up in a revolution.')

The plea of the Fiscal, Mr Denyssen, makes fascinating, if nauseating, reading.

'Worshipful gentlemen,' he opens his address to the court, 'it is a lamentable truth which experience has taught us, that when once the idea of being oppressed has entered into and taken root in the human mind, whether groundless or not, it will oftentimes carry men to unthought of extremities'— extremities amply demonstrated in South Africa in 1976 and 1977.

The Fiscal insists that what he says should not be construed as an apology for slavery (today's Foreign Minister Pik Botha is just as eloquent in his views on discrimination). Nevertheless, he points out that the stability of Cape society is based on the assumption that free men and slaves all accept their prescribed place and function in that society.

'As long as every man is satisfied with his station in life, peace and contentment reign in the mind, and no rupture of the existing tranquillity is to be feared, however unequal the situation of the one may be from that of the other.

159

'But scarcely does man feel that his inequality with those whom fortune has placed in more favourable circumstances affords him reason of discontent, and that he conceives he has to bear a burden which is unjustly imposed on him, than his passions begin to work, peace is banished from his mind, and he will leave nothing to find an opportunity to throw off his load.'

Sharpeville was to Soweto what the uprising of 1808 had been to that of 1824: 'The country in which we live,' declaims Denyssen, 'has, alas! already in our time afforded more than one proof of this truth, and Heaven protect us from witnessing any more.' (Which, as it turned out, Heaven didn't.)

Like Mr B. J. Vorster a century and a half later, the Fiscal states the morality of his case before the world: 'Taught by the moral lessons of our Holy Religion to obey their masters, they did not withdraw themselves from this obedience without well knowing to have failed in their duty; and the punishment of their offence left no other impression on their minds than that they had brought it on themselves by their own bad conduct.'

The voice of Law and Order is very emphatic on this point: 'This impression was necessary as tending to observe order and tranquillity in the Land.'

Of course, the true motive behind this high-minded morality very soon becomes apparent. And it is, not surprisingly, a matter of basic economics. The free inhabitants of the Colony, the Fiscal points out, have not only been allowed by law but actively encouraged by the authorities 'to invest a very important part of their means and their welfare in the purchase of slaves. Under such circumstances that impression by which slaves are bound to obey their masters was and is absolutely necessary for the good order and well being of the state.'

Having now established, via the tortuous route from morality to economics, the imperative of state security, the

160

Fiscal cannot but lament the fact that 'some evil, disposed and wicked persons, whose evident object was to involve the whole Country in Anarchy and Confusion,' started indoctrinating well-meaning slaves. Thus, by holding up to these unfortunate creatures the fact that England herself was free of slavery, the local slaves were, in Mr Denyssen's view, unscrupulously goaded towards demanding the same condition for their own country.

Inherent in this reasoning is the same Protestant ethic which inspired Minister C. P. Mulder when earlier this year he tried to defend the heinous implications of the new proposed legislation to gag the press.

Using the rather stale image of the fish allowed complete freedom to swim as it wishes provided it stays in the water, the Minister really brought across very forcibly the fact that any slave is as free as his master chooses him to be.

There is one elementary mistake in this reasoning, and that is that a man is not a fish. Man can think, a fish cannot; man knows his condition, a fish doesn't. And because, unlike Dr Mulder, I have a higher regard for a man than for a fish, I demand for man rather more than for a fish.

In the heart of the matter, the Fiscal observes, quite rightly resounds 'the cry of murder at the disappointed hope for freedom, raised by a slave'. This links up, unexpectedly, with a statement in a stimulating essay 'The Violent Reverie', by Professor Noel Chabani Manganyi of Umtata University; exploring Camus's argument in *The Myth of Sisyphus*, he suggests an essential difference between black and white (read: slave and master) in a situation like the present.

The white, he says, operates in the dimension of the metaphysical and contemplates the existential problem of suicide. But the black Sisyphus, coming downhill to face his truth, operates exclusively in the dimension of the social: his rock is murder, not suicide.

The Fiscal, obviously, finds neither justification nor mitigation for rebellion in thwarted hopes of liberty, because these very hopes place the security of the state in jeopardy. Arguing, like many a Nationalist Cabinet Minister in recent times, that 'the slave is almost as safe under the protection of his Master as the child under that of the father,' Denyssen regards aspirations towards liberation as the most pernicious of all crimes. 'The eagerness to shake off the yoke of slavery . . . cannot be considered in any other light than a desire to withdraw themselves from the laws of the land and from obedience to Government.'

In his view the urge for freedom is simply the equivalent of 'a desire for blood, war and confusion leading to the most disastrous anarchy'—a confirmation of moral and political myopia South Africa has witnessed all too often recently. And so the Fiscal concludes that 'the desire for freedom thus directed is a reason for the aggravation of the punishment.'

So it comes as no surprise that the leaders of the rebellion were sentenced to death and their heads exposed on iron spikes in 'the most conspicuous places in the Bokkeveld, there to remain till consumed by time and the birds of the air'.

But the revolt as such, like the motivation behind it, has NOT been consumed by time. And it is part of the horror of the South African situation in 1978 that the slave-owner mentality exemplified in the case of 1825, still forms a main ingredient in the social and political thinking of this Government.

Mapmakers

(1978)

I

Inside every writer is a word struggling to get out.

This word embodies the writer's perception of the world, of what he has seen, of what he fervently believes to be true. And so every time this word is uttered the possibility exists for a small particle of truth to be set free into the world where it can communicate with others.

At the same time, however, there is a chance that truth may be falsified or distorted or narrowed down in the process because in this guise truth—which in itself is vast and non-verbal—has to assume the form of language: and not even language in general, as part of a social and acceptable code, but the language of an individual, a relative, uncertain, undependable, disreputable man. And yet the writer, however constantly he may be humbled by his encounters with truth and with the world, is also an arrogant creature, and must be so in order to survive: he must have the presumption to believe in the possibility that the word he sets free, however limited or warped it may be, contains enough of the truth to warrant its liberation. Otherwise he will not, and cannot, write at all.

Deep inside him he apprehends a welter and a whorl of

truth, a great confounding darkness which he shapes into a word; surrounding him is the light of freedom into which his word is sent like a dove from the ark. In this way, through the act of writing, truth and liberty communicate. Of course, the writer is not the only medium through whom truth can be let loose into the world: the scientist does it in his own way, and the philosopher in his; every human being is involved in the same process—but the writer is unique in his peculiar involvement with the word.

II

Every writer chooses the particular way in which to set free his word, which is his self. To a large extent it may be an act of free choice; but in many ways, obviously, his temperament, his inclination, his experience, his overall condition, may determine that choice. However, once one has made the necessary allowance for the personality and situation of the individual writer, the nature of his choice can really be influenced only by a consideration of the social and/or cultural climate in which he operates.

In the relatively open society, i.e. the society in which the whole alphabet of human experience from A to Z is accessible to the writer and where the whole alphabet of expression from A to Z is at his disposal, the very extent of his freedom may diminish the weight of what he has to say. After all, if he is free to say (and if his public knows that he is free to say) anything from A to Z, why should any particular significance be attached to the fact that he elects to say B or M or X rather than C or Q or P?

In the closed society on the other hand, where the writer is allowed only the freedom to pronounce the letters from A to M, his word immediately acquires a peculiar weight if he risks not only his comfort but his personal security in choosing to say N, or V, or Z. Because of the risk involved, his word acquires a new resonance: it ceases, in fact, to be 'merely' a word and enters the world as an act in its own right.

A critic from a relatively free society (the US, Britain, France, Sweden . . .) sometimes feels himself obliged to ask, 'But surely it cannot be enough merely to write?' The background to his scepticism is a society in which 'mere writing' has often been experienced as a way of opting out, of choosing to write rather than to 'do something', of self-indulgence rather than commitment. Now, obviously, being a writer can never exempt the individual from his duties and responsibilities as a citizen; at the same time, within the context of a repressive society, writing can—and does—become an act not of turning one's back on the world but of fully immersing oneself in it.

This does not make him a captive of his situation. There is a peculiar experience of liberty operating in these circumstances: that liberty which is activated when what a man *wants* to do coincides with what, not only morally but existentially, he feels himself *obliged* to do. Of the Jew in the Warsaw ghetto during the Second World War it was *expected* that he should revolt: in order to preserve not only his dignity but in fact his life he had no choice but to revolt. At the same time, caught up in that particular situation as an individual, his own personal priority, his own most ardent wish, would have been to revolt. The historical imperative and the individual urge coincided, determining a new and ex-hilarating experience of liberty. The same would apply to the suppressed black man in South Africa. And it applies, too, to the writer who finds himself beleaguered in a state of oppression. When the conspiracy of lies surrounding me demands of me to silence the one word of truth given to me, *that word becomes the one word I wish to utter above all others*: and at the same time it is the word my metaphysical situation, my historical situation, and my own craft demand of me to utter.

In such a situation the writer may be acclaimed by some and crucified by others: but whatever happens *he is not ignored*. This, in turn, imposes a heavy responsibility on his conscience. For if everything he says is going to make some impact on his environment, he has to weigh doubly every word he utters in order to make as sure as is humanly possible that his perception and his account of the world is as true as he is able to render it.

III

There are two metaphors I can think of to express the function of the writer in a repressive society. Both have to do with mapmaking, and in a sense they may appear to be mutually exclusive. Yet I believe both are valid.

The first comes from the apocryphal journal of a Danish explorer, one Christian Frederick Damberger, alleged to have visited the Cape of Good Hope in the late eighteenth century. Before venturing into the interior he tried to find a reliable map of the territory which, at that stage, was still, to a large extent, *terra incognita*. His enquiries led him to a certain corporal Martens on the False Bay coast at Muizenberg. The episode is best described in Damberger's own words:

> In the garrison at the Meisenberg was a corporal named Martens . . . who having accompanied Colonel Gordon in a journey inland as far as Caffraria, had laid down a map of the country, and sent it to the company [i.e. the Dutch East India Company, governors of the Cape] in expectation of receiving a handsome reward: but he only received an order never to draw another, if he wished to avoid being condemned to thirty years' imprisonment. This, however, did not deter him from pursuing his labours, and he frequently applied himself with his door locked to completing his map. I sought his friendship, and soon obtained it; but he always hid his papers as soon as I came. Once, however, I said to him that I well knew

166

what he was drawing, but that he had no reason to fear I should betray him, for I was extremely fond of such pursuits, and he would do me the greatest favour by shewing me a map of the interior of the country. This request indeed he refused, but permitted me to take copies of his other drawings Upon this I immediately set to work, and found that these studies assisted me much in preparation for the execution of my project.

The parallel is startlingly obvious. The strange territory explored and mapped for the first time; the assiduous cartographer offering his map to the world and threatened, to his dismay, with thirty years in chains should he disclose it; and the long lonely years afterwards, during which he continues to draw and redraw his map, refining it all the time in order to correspond more and more closely to the land he has explored. Here is the writer slaving away in his ceaseless attempt to draw the map of his vision of truth, risking his liberty in order to offer to the world a view of itself. And, opposing him, is a government prepared to go to any extremes in order to keep the truth locked away.

There is something absurd in the situation. To the government's realistic and pragmatic threat of thirty years in chains the cartographer offers no practical answer: all he does is to go on drawing map after map, in secret. It would seem that the most he can hope for is the discovery of his map by someone else, some time in the distant future, possibly after his own death. And yet it must have seemed sufficient reward to him simply to carry on drawing. Inevitably, one is reminded of Nadezhda Mandelshtam committing to memory, for thirty years, her husband's poems before she finally found the opportunity of publishing them. Truth will out.

IV

A vision of truth also inspires the second metaphor which expresses, for me, the *raison d'être* of the writer. Once more a map is involved, but this time the map of an imaginary land, a strange and distant but necessary Kingdom of Monomotapa which Gorky called Virtue and which we can call Truth.

In *The Lower Depths* the old man Luka tells the story of a poor man living in Siberia and keeping himself alive through his desperate belief in a Virtuous Land. ' . . . whenever things got so bad for him that he might just as well lie down and die, he'd never lose heart, he'd just smile to himself and he'd say, "It's nothing. I can bear it, I'll just hang on a bit longer and then I'll be away, away from all this, away to the virtuous land."'

Then, one day, an exiled scientist arrived in Siberia, carrying with him all the paraphernalia of his trade: books and plans and maps and instruments. The poor man hurried to the scientist and asked him to show him, on his maps, the location of that mythical Virtuous Land. Of course, the scientist did the contrary: he showed him proof that such a land existed nowhere in the known world. In a frenzy, the poor man insisted that the land must exist: if not, '"all your books and maps are completely worthless."' When the scientist persisted, the poor man was desperate: '"Oh you swine," he said, "you're a crook not a scientist!" And with that he fetched the scientist a clout across the ear, and then another across the other . . . Then he went home and hanged himself.'

The writer, instead of hanging himself, turns to his own paper and draws, himself, the map of the Land of Truth he knows exists in himself.

I do not wish for one moment to suggest, as countless schools of didactic and 'uplifting' literature have done, that the writer should soothe his audience with lies about a non-existent utopia; that he should pretend that the world is a

168

better place to live in than he knows it to be; that he should turn his back on the real and change his art into a palliative, a new opium for the masses.

But I do think one can reconcile Gorky's image with Damberger's. The writer is not concerned only with 're-producing' the real. What he does is to perceive, below the lines of the map he draws, the contours of another world, somehow a more 'essential' world. And from the interaction between the land as he *perceives* it to be and the land as he knows it *can* be, someone from outside, the 'reader' of the map, watches—and aids—the emergence of the *meaning* of the map.

V

It remains a map: it is not the world itself. It offers no protection against the rigours of the world: the heat or rain, wild animals, rivers in flood, an unremitting sun. If it is essential for survival, it is essential on another level of existence altogether.

The point is—to change the metaphor—that the writer, as a writer, cannot wield the same weapons as his adversaries. Whatever he does as a person, as a citizen of his state, is something else. But when he takes up the challenges which confront him as a *writer*, he does so in a dimension different from that of politicians and soldiers. A book cannot enter the field of battle against a sword. If the book does win in the end, as I am convinced, the reason for its final victory lies in the very fact that it declines to resort to the same sort of weapons as its adversaries.

It follows that even when the writer chooses socio-political experience as his battlefield, his approach and mode of action are radically different from those of the politician or the pamphleteer. Even in his commitment he does not debase his art to the level of practical politics: instead, if he is really serious about his trade as a writer, he probes and examines and refines even politics in such a way that it becomes valid as aesthetic experience.

Many people tend to regard the writer in such a context as impotent: how on earth can he expect to achieve anything against the battalions lined up against him? The rub lies in the very choice of words: in 'achieve'. For the writer simply cannot weigh his achievement on any practical scale: it belongs to a different order. To assess his work in terms of immediate 'effect' would be both senseless and futile. In this lies the hell of the writer's task: and if he is not prepared to come to terms with it he should abandon writing. If, on the other hand, he does accept this condition and aims at other things (if he aims, at most, at changing insights and sensibilities, at effecting his subtle revolution within the hearts and minds of individuals), his very hell may turn into his heaven too. (And it is not for nothing that I clothe this argument in religious terms: Kafka was, I believe, one of the first to find in art a form of 'secular religion' in a world which had lost both faith and trust in other things.)

The true response of the writer to his situation lies in not allowing literature to be turned into anything else. To produce literature—nothing more than literature, but certainly nothing less than literature either—is the highest he can demand of himself. Which means that, whether he writes about the agony or about the ecstasy of experience, about love or disillusionment, about silence or violence, about history or the contemporary scene, about private fears or the socio-political dimension of man, the writer's primary concern is with the quality of his work. Nothing may be allowed to interfere with that or dictate to that: even anger should be distilled into something permanent. Then, and only then, his small word of truth becomes not so much an outcry *against* something as an affirmation and celebration of something: above all, of that humiliated, maligned, exploited, suppressed, fragile, frail, forked creature—*man*.

To the question of poor Katja 'What shall I do?' we can answer only [say Thomas Mann] with the words 'Upon my honour and conscience I do not know.' We work none the less, we tell tales, give them form, and entertain a needy world in the dark hope, almost in the confidence, that truth and serene form are able to make an impact which grants spiritual freedom and that they are thus able to prepare the world for a life which is better, more beautiful and more appropriate to the human spirit.

We may have lost much of the faith in a 'better world' which inspired Mann (and which Gorky's Luka would have loved to believe in)—between us and them lie worlds and World Wars and the shipwreck of many certainties—but by continuing to write, unintimidated and without compromise, we can still keep alive the faith in more liberty than we know at present, in more justice, in more morality. In the quality of the writer's work, in the closeness with which his map approaches the truth of the geography he has observed and which he believes in, in the intensity and integrity of his moral and aesthetic response to the violence and the indignities of the world, we can discover something of our dangerous salvation. In a world of centrifugal forces the writer can patiently, humbly and inexorably continue his search for centres of gravity. In a world of disintegration he can express his allegiance to sense and coherence in the integration of his own work. In a time when official history marches with great boots across the prostrate and humiliated body of truth, he can side with those who, in Camus's words, undergo this process. In a world where the lie is celebrated, the writer can sustain truth by refusing to put away his maps and by risking thirty years in chains for the sake of setting free that truth—sometime, somehow.

171

The Writer in
a State of Siege

(1979)

I

To the beleaguered situation of the writer in South Africa today there are at least two stock responses, each as futile as the other. While some appear to revel in the idea of martyrdom, others prefer to shrug it off with an attitude of: 'Why worry? Writers have always been persecuted. We'll get through somehow.'

I propose a third alternative: action, both individual and collective, to meet the challenges of the situation.

In order to weigh the possibilities inherent in this choice it would be useful to approach the situation in this country today within as broad a perspective as possible. By looking at threats posed to writers in different countries and at different moments in history, we may derive from the responses of our peers and predecessors an insight into at least some of the tactics that ensured the survival of the species, endangered as it may appear to be.

For obvious reasons I shall limit myself to threats posed to writers through the ages by various established forms of authority which had at their command sufficient power to curtail the writer's existential freedom to write and to communicate. It is a situation in which some configuration of the concepts power, freedom, reality and truth perenially recur.

'The sin of power,' wrote Arthur Miller in an article with that title, 'is not only to distort reality but to convince people that the false is true, and that what is happening is only an invention of enemies.' This predicament defines the possible function of the writer: 'A road—sometimes merely a narrow path—always remained open before my mind, the belief that I might sensibly attempt to influence people to see what was real and so at least to resist the victory of untruth.'

What is at stake, is not just the individual writer's grasp of reality, or his freedom to write, but by implication an entire community's access to reality and truth. This is the major argument of Julio Cortazar in 'Something more than Words':

> It is true that we writers always find a way of writing and even publishing, but on the other side of the wall there are readers who cannot read without taking risks; on the other side are people whose only source of information is the official one; on the other side there is a generation of children and adolescents who . . . are 'educated' to become perfect fascists, automatic defenders of the big words that disguise reality: fatherland, national security, discipline, God . . .

The curators of these noble-sounding lies are those in power—a power which is narcissist by nature, striving constantly to perpetuate itself through cloning, approaching more and more a state of utter homogeneity by casting out whatever seems foreign or deviant, until all the parts become interchangeable and reflect perfectly the whole. Power tends by nature to reduce points of reference and support outside itself in order to gain autonomy and be self-sufficient. We have experienced enough of all this in South Africa over the years; just as we have seen more than enough of the distortion of reality through lies; of the obstacles placed in the way of simple truths subjected to expedience; and of that arrogance which is the stamp of absolute power. (An arrogance which expresses itself by being 'left cold' by whatever happens outside, no matter how bloody or inhuman; an arrogance which concedes as a person's only democratic right the right to die, in the winged words of Minister of Justice (!) Jimmy Kruger when he referred to the death of Steve Biko.)

These are the given elements of the context within which we are to explore the writer's resistance to oppression.

II

Anyone discussing writers in a state of siege does so in the shadow of two great Greeks: Socrates (archetype of the writer, even though he himself wrote down no word), who chose the poison cup above exile after being found guilty of harming the morals of the young, and who, in the month between his sentence and his execution, continued, unperturbed, to teach his disciples; and Plato, who could find no room for the poet in his Ideal Republic.

It would seem that Plato's attitude was decisive in many times and countries, ranging from the actions of the Chinese emperor Shih Huang To who, in the 3rd century BC built the Great Wall (to ward off enemies within) . . . to the notorious book-burnings of Hitler; and from ancient Persia, where writers whose work offended the king were forced to lick the ink from their manuscripts to present-day regimes in the Philippines, or Indonesia, or South America, or Africa, where writers are jailed and/or tortured in many ways.

Yet in spite of this the writer has managed to survive, a phoenix of innumerable avatars and metamorphoses. What concerns us is the ways in which writers reacted to oppression or to threats. In this respect the primary motivation of the writer has always been that expressed by the great Russian sculptor Neizvestny who is reported by John Berger to have won an explosive argument with Khruschev by shouting:

'You may be Premier and Chairman, but not here in front of my works. Here I am Premier and we shall discuss as equals.'

It was this same Neizvestny who, when asked how on earth he found it possible to resist so much pressure from the State, replied: 'There are certain bacteria—very small, soft ones— which can live in a supersaline solution that could dissolve the hoof of a rhinoceros.' (Also cited by Berger, in *Art and Revolution*.)

III

There is not much point in going back too far in history, since the writer in ancient Greece or during the Middle Ages fulfilled a function so different from the one he exercised in, say, the Renaissance or afterwards that it is practically impossible to find natural analogies with the situation today. (It is significant too, that the *Index Librorum Prohibitorum* coincided with the advent of Renaissance and Reformation!) Practically all literature produced before the discovery of the printing press existed as forms of *zamishdat avant la lettre*, copied and distributed privately, and consequently difficult to control; and during the Middle Ages even this form of restricted publication was dependent almost exclusively on the system of patronage. A writer simply couldn't afford to publish his work unless it had been approved by his patron, a procedure clearly encouraging the distribution of 'acceptable' versions of the truth.

Even so, a few observations about that distant past may not be amiss. Commendable in ancient Greece was the notion of *parrhesia*, the freedom to speak your mind both in public and in private. In practice, of course, it was restricted by the unfortunate fact that only privileged citizens had any interest in exploiting it (and even among them there was the sobering reminder of Socrates!). Those who transgressed in speech or writing the common-law prescriptions governing decency, libel, etc. were banished, which was the logical form of punishment in a society with largely oral traditions in literature. And what happened to Aristophanes or Euripides illustrates both the extent of tolerance and the efficacy of banishment in the ancient world. Remove the offending speaker and he is automatically silenced. Which was what the judges meant to do to Socrates, only he refused to go.

Rome also found it a convenient way of dealing with outspokenness, as Ovid discovered. But what concerns us more than the action taken by the authorities is his reaction to it. In exile in Pontus he wrote his greatest works, the *Tristia* and the *Epistulae ex Ponto*, copies of which filtered back to the ungrateful fatherland. And when all copies of his earlier work were removed from public libraries, they continued to circulate privately. In spite of an embarrassing, if understandable, tone of supplication in his later work, there was one area in which he refused to make any concessions: 'Over poetry the emperor has no say,' he insisted, an attitude borne out by the continued circulation of his writings.

Not that Rome was really so intolerant. The most vulgar abuse could be heaped on any emperor safely dead: only the ruler in power had to be treated with deference, which explains why Seneca, Tacitus and Suetonius all managed to do their work in relative comfort. And even when the ruling emperor was insulted, action against the author was usually taken only if his work was circulated in public: no attempt, it seems, was made to confiscate private copies.

This attitude persisted throughout the Middle Ages and well into the Renaissance, except that the Church took over most of the function of censorship from the State. Where the State continued to occupy itself with such matters (as in Britain, where all theatrical performances had to be licensed by an official bearing the precious title of *Master of Revels* or *Lord of Misrule*) it acted in close conjunction with the Church and, in later years, as its 'protector'.

The most illustrious name from this period is that of

Dante, although his death sentence, imposed during an absence on a diplomatic mission to Rome, had nothing to do with his writing. Even so, his reaction to the sentence is of some relevance to us: when he embarked on the composition of the *Divina Commedia* in Bologna, he relegated all his adversaries to hell.

IV

The first few centuries after the discovery of printing brought about significant changes in the situation of the writer, changes highlighted especially by developments in Britain.

'In the interests of the safety of the State' British kings assumed an absolute prerogative over the printing of anything from pamphlet to book, a form of pre-publication censorship through licensing which put the writer in a particularly precarious position. Then, as now, much of the problem was caused by the very vagueness of terms like 'seditious words', 'unfitting worddes', 'unsemely words' or 'evil opinions'; and things were hardly improved by the preponderance of churchmen involved in the application of censorship, a practice which places South Africa firmly within the context of the late Middle Ages.

Add to this the consideration that Henry VIII held 'forged tydings and tales' in particular contempt, and it will be readily understood that the writer or playwright of the time was at a disadvantage even before he committed words to paper. Still, for the sake of equilibrium, one should remind those who are so ready to point out that 'Shakespeare managed to write what he did in spite of stringent censorship', that 'undesirability' in his time was seen almost exclusively in terms of the likelihood of giving offence to the Church or the King. In fact, Puritans experienced more trouble than anyone else in obtaining licences!—in 1593, for instance, one Mr Stubbes complained bitterly:

I cannot but lament the corruption of our time, for alas now-a-
days it is grown to be a hard matter to get a good book licensed
without staying, peradventure, a quarter of a year for it; yea,
sometimes two or three years before he have it allowed, and in
the end happly rejected too; so that that which many a good man
hath . . . ravailed long in shall . . . never see the light;
whilst . . . other bookes, full of al filthines, scurrility, baudry,
dissoluteness, cosenage, conycatching and the like . . . are
either quickly licensed, or at least easily tollerated.

Since 1557 the Stationers' Company held the monopoly of
printing in Britain; in addition, every manuscript first had to
be passed by a selection committee appointed jointly by
Church and State. In spite of all this, as we know only too
well, writing flourished in Elizabethan times. There were
innumerable loopholes. One might follow Shakespeare's
example and obtain the protection of important patrons
against others; or one might disguise the tensions of the
present in the patterns of history, both British and foreign, in
order to make oneself heard very clearly by those who knew
what to listen for. Otherwise one might follow the example of
Marlowe or his successors Dryden and Milton and others, by
turning to the clandestine press. If prescriptions abounded,
control was deficient; and most people in authority tended to
turn a blind eye, unlike those administering censorship in
South Africa today.

In an excellent article on the freedom of the press Robert
Birley writes: 'What was learnt in these days was the
technique of subversive literature, the printing of it in secret,
the use of colporteurs to spread it, the use of false imprints in
books to put investigators off the scent, the smuggling of
books from abroad . . . ' Countless French books were
printed in Britain or the Netherlands; and countless English
books in France. Sometimes English books were printed in
England itself, stamped with the imprint of a foreign
publisher to fool the censors (cf. the priceless 'Douai'

publications from those times). And the very monopoly of the Stationers' Company sent large numbers of private printers scavenging through the country, offering their services to any writer who had something to say and a few pence to pay for it.

Such writers found their justification in an eloquent statement by Giacomo Contio in 1565: ' . . . the idea that truth should be maintained by the power of civil authorities [is] simply ridiculous. The search for truth must begin with doubt; the road to truth lies through free discussion; once freedom is established truth will in the end prevail.' These words provide an answer to critics who are always eager to accuse the writer of arrogance, as if he were pretending to be the sole custodian of truth in the world. Clearly no writer, no individual, has a monopoly on 'the truth'. But only by acknowledging doubt and allowing fearless and free discussion can people begin to move towards some perception of truth. And in the end this truth will out, whatever efforts are made to inhibit or stifle it. Can one afford to forget Milton's delightful image in the *Areopagitica* (1644) in which he compared censorship to 'that gallant man who thought to pound up the crows by shutting his Park gate'?

Milton's great French contemporary Molière did not find writing a bed of roses either, not even when he had the Roi Soleil on his side (which, in itself, was one way of getting one's own thing done): if he still enjoyed enough freedom to reply to the scandal following *L'Ecole des Femmes* with the piercing wit of *La Critique de l'Ecole des Femmes* and *L'Impromptu de Versailles*, all possibility of public retaliation was denied him when it came to his greatest works. All public performances of *Tartuffe* were banned in 1664. But instead of yielding to pressure Molière reacted by producing *Don Juan*, which caused an even greater scandal. For the next five years he did all he could to persuade the king to lift the ban, which finally happened in 1669.

In the meantime his contemporary John Bunyan had

begun to demonstrate yet another response to persecution, an archetypical writer's response at that: condemned to twelve years' imprisonment when he refused to give up offering church services in defiance of the prescriptions of the Church of England, he wrote his most important work in jail: *Grace Abounding* and, most especially, *The Pilgrim's Progress*, in which, like Dante before him, he elevated personal experience to universal allegory.

A completely different reaction to a situation of siege came from Voltaire during a particularly dark phase of the Enlightenment. Like his English counterparts Swift, Addison and Steele, the rapier Voltaire preferred to use in his defence was ridicule, satire, wit: but Voltaire was too much of a virtuoso to employ only one weapon. He found a particularly astute—and very French—solution after his *Lettres Philosophiques* (1734) had landed him in trouble: moving in with the powerful Madame du Châtelet and entering into a liaison with her, he felt safe enough to go on writing as before, knowing that her power was sufficient to keep at bay even the Roi Soleil. As an added precaution he pretended to have his work printed in Kehl (although, in fact, it was all done in France). Whatever could be confiscated of what he wrote in those years was burned, with or without ceremony, which in itself enhanced the value of his books. Some Inspectors of the Book Trade were known to stow away the copies of his work they could lay hands on, in anticipation of selling them at a profit in the future. (Throughout the long history of censorship this has remained one of the more positive side-effects of the whole depressing business. As Richard Carlile said in 1831: 'A prosecution becomes the grand impetus for reading a particular book, and in the language of Thomas Pains I say again, "May every good book be prosecuted."')

When things finally became too hot for Voltaire he resorted to the immemorial remedy of exile. Not without irony, for having left Catholic France he soon invited the wrath of Geneva's fervent Calvinists. The only solution lay in retiring to Ferney where, in an age of intolerance, he continued to pour forth his message of tolerance. In the final analysis the lesson of Voltaire, as of all the other writers in our catalogue, lies in the fact that no discomfort, danger, prosecution or exile could force him into silence.

V

In the wake of the taking of the Bastille came the Declaration of Human and Citizen Rights with its emphasis on 'The free communication of thoughts and opinions [which] is one of the individual's most precious rights: therefore every citizen may speak, write and print freely, provided that in those cases prescribed by law he shall have to justify any misuse of this freedom.'

Alas, in practice it did not work out quite so well for writers, especially in the years following the Congress of Vienna when most European governments clamped down very severely on dissident intellectuals—in most cases for political and other public reasons, in some cases for more personal ones. But once again, what concerns us most is the fact that neither political pamphleteers jailed for their writings nor poets, novelists or playwrights persecuted in a variety of spectacular, if less excessive, ways in the course of the nineteenth century were persuaded to fall silent. At least one of them—Strindberg—went mad but this may have happened in any case (it followed upon a prosecution for blasphemy): what is significant is that his most important work was written *afterwards*. Ibsen left his country in disgust ('My country knows no freedom: only smaller freedoms'—which, presumably, South Africans would translate as 'separate freedoms'): even after his eventual triumphant return he remained the rebel to the very end, when he died pronouncing the defiant word: *Tvertimut*—'On the contrary!'—which is the writer's motto *par excellence*.

With Ibsen we have already crossed the threshold into our

own century. And what irony that the country which in 1900 promised more than any other the inspiring vision of a New Humanity, Russia, should so soon become synonymous with the worst suppression and persecution of writers and the worst oppression of the truth the world has ever known? The twentieth century has become an age of new dictatorships— Right as well as Left—that do their utmost consciously to silence truth or to distort it, or to cover it up with lies: because, to a greater extent than ever before, ideologies and mass values are threatening the voice of the individual.

Yet it has not yet happened, not totally. From the inexhaustible supply of examples from the chronicles of our century, a brief series of case histories should be illuminating.

The Weimar Republic and the Third Reich: for years writers struggled to survive in the country, doing their best to make themselves heard through public protests, deputations, congresses. But by 1933 they had to acknowledge that a crossroads had been reached. After the burning of the Reichstag Hitler blamed the intellectuals (both communist and anti-communist) for what had happened. It inspired the great *autos-da-fé*, the arrests, the systematic persecution. The result was not the general silence he had hoped for but a mass exodus of leading writers (among them Brecht and Heinrich and Thomas Mann), regrouping themselves in other countries—Switzerland, France, Holland, the USA—from where a properly organized literature-in-exile was launched.

'Emigration,' said Heinrich Mann in 1934, 'is the voice of a nation that has fallen silent.'

Accused of stabbing Germany in the back and betraying the nation (accusations all too familiar to Afrikaans writers, even though their conditions are not nearly comparable yet), Thomas Mann replied in 1937: 'I am supposed to have insulted the Reich and wounded Germany by rebelling

182

against it. They have the incredible audacity to confuse themselves with Germany!'—followed in 1939 by the wonderful arrogance and the simple truth of another brief statement: 'Wherever I am, Germany is.' Because nowhere, and in no other way, can a nation be represented so authentically as in the work of its best writers—even when, on the surface, that work appears to attack or condemn the fatherland.

Elsewhere in Europe too, wherever the eagle spread its sombre wings and left the swastika imprint of its claws, writers were making themselves heard, their presence felt. Even inside a German camp the Dutch writer Vestdijk never interrupted his writing, calmly producing his self-imposed daily quota in a quiet but irresistible manifestation of dignity in the face of degradation. And right under the eyes of the German occupiers and their Vichy collaborators French writers like Anouilh (*Antigone*) and Sartre (*Les Mouches*), to name but two, 'rewrote' classical Greek plays to become the vehicles of their profound resistance. In their situation the classics became masks—transparent to their audiences, but apparently incomprehensible to the German overlords—of the attitude of an entire nation. In spite of the constant danger of execution Camus and Beckett also continued to write in their respective hiding-places, concerned above all by the *quality* of their work, and, in the case of Camus, by the urge to lend a voice to all the voiceless oppressed of the war. There is but one way a writer can do his work in our time, said Camus, and that is: *écrire dangereusement*.

VI

In the period since the war the territories which concern us most are the countries behind the Iron Curtain, and the Third World.

What has been written about Romania can be applied to

many other countries: the emergence, after 1945, of two distinct groups of writers; those, like Sadoveaunu, Călinescu, etc. who allowed themselves to be bridled and turned into 'praise writers'; and those like Blaga, Barbu, Voiculescu, etc. who began to write only 'for the drawer'. This continued at least until after the death of Stalin, when cautious publication recommenced: 'Writers learned the secrets of the parable (books with a clue)', explained one commentator, 'and of "partial truth" (or more precisely: truth by the drop)'. Another phase began in 1977 with the abolition of bureaucratic censorship, to be replaced by something even more diabolical, for now *writers* were appointed to judge the work of their peers—a refinement recently made available to South African quislings as well. In the words of one Romanian writer: 'Writers become censors are more ruthless with their colleagues' manuscripts than the professional censors . . . A writer does not hesitate to condemn a fellow-writer's work—one who has travelled to the West more often than himself, one who earns more, or who has won a prize that was refused him, or who, yesterday at the café, said about him that . . . '

In Hungary, too, legal censorship was eventually abolished: but only because publishers were kept so much under control that they could be trusted to do the Government's work for it. (Do we not have experience of this too?) The result, as reported from inside, is that more and more good work is turned down for publication and condemned to the drawer. Here, as in Romania, there is a growing demand for *zamishdat*. But unlike the USSR where *zamishdat* has acquired a considerable reputation since practically all significant dissident work is distributed in that form, most leading Hungarian authors are reported to hesitate before taking such a decisive step—for the obvious reason that official censorship has been abolished. They seem to prefer to hold back, hoping that one day it will be possible for their work to be published in the normal way.

Their reluctance is depriving more and more possible readers of alternatives to that pernicious 'official' truth which prevails in authoritarian societies. To counter this, a small group of leading intellectuals led by Janos Kĕnedi have started the semi-clandestine publication *Profile*: work which has no hope of being published in Hungary, is smuggled out of the country, mainly to England, where it is published, usually in the original. There appear to be interesting parallels between *Profile* and *Taurus* in South Africa, which offers an 'honourable' means of publication to the writer whose work is regarded as too dangerous for publication by the larger, established publishers—without going all the way underground. At the same time it offers an opportunity of self-defence to writers who, otherwise, can be too easily discredited merely on the strength of rumour.

For several years after the war writers in Czechoslovakia also 'wrote for the drawer' before they began to risk publishing their work. According to Dušan Hamšik, most of those efforts were very cautious and ambiguous indeed, in an effort 'to come round to those touchy and painful problems of the present day by *apparently* ignoring them. We proposed to seek their roots in the past, either in authentic history or in that pseudo-history which preserves them in the national consciousness . . . ' In due course even that was banned. The writers reacted, once again according to Hamšik, with 'allegorical statements describing reality in a secret code of vague hints and absurdities'. Several of the greatest writers left after 1968: Škvorecký, Keundera, Lustig . . . Among those who remained behind, some slowly became more confident, more audacious, resulting in a direct confrontation with the authorities with the appearance of *Charter 77*. The result, as we know only too well, was complete 'defeat' in the short term—but if world opinion and the sheer courage of Czech writers themselves are any indication, it must inevitably lead to victory in the long run. Even extremely authoritarian regimes remain curiously sensitive about the particular sort of international scandal caused by a clampdown on dissidents (however much the authorities may pretend, for the time being, to be un-flappable).

Several years before *Charter 77* Czech writers had launched the remarkable publication *Padlock*. Edited by Ludvik Vaculík, it has already brought into circulation more than a hundred works in the form of *tamishdat* (publication abroad), to be smuggled back into Czechoslovakia from outside, where the printing is done. (The scope of this venture is augmented by brisk circulation in *zamishdat*, as well as by publication—in English as well as the original Czech—in London.) For a long time the authorities refrained from acting against contributors to *Padlock*, reserving their repressive measures for readers caught with copies in their possession. The arrest of the poet Jiri Grusa in 1978 appeared to mark a turning point in this particular history; but the international outcry caused by it was so enormous that the Czech authorities received at least a severe moral dent in the process. They may be reluctant to repeat the exercise: but even if they do (and for the time being they may feel obliged to flex their muscles just to 'prove' that they are not intimidated) Grusa and his colleagues have already impressed the world with what, at the 1978 Congress of PEN in Stockholm, Kohout and Vaclav (*in absentia*) termed 'the indivisibility of freedom and . . . our re-sponsibility to it'.

In China the leading novelist is reported to be Pa Chin, who was discredited by the Cultural Revolution after enjoying tremendous popularity in the 1930s and 1940s. For ten years he had to scrub the floors in the offices of the Writers' Union and clean their latrines. After Mao's death he was freed—for the life of a political regime is limited, however durable it may appear at the time; and a writer's word outlasts it—and in a new novel he exposed everything he had lived through: 'I want to accuse and to express my

indignation.' But even during the clamp-down on writers by
Mao's regime their silence was not total: in a time when
practically nothing but Mao's own work was allowed to be
distributed thousands of poems, short stories and apparently
even novels were circulated *orally*. From reports at first hand
it would seem that this form of communication became part
of an entire new community culture. At tea ceremonies these
works would be recited, and everybody in the company
would be invited to make their own contribution to the
developing whole: which, of course, closely resembles the
emergence of the earliest sagas and epics of our culture. And
it certainly is significant that this particular form of oral
zamishdat is prevalent in the black community in South
Africa today: where the written word can be readily traced to a
writer, who can then be prosecuted or intimidated, the
spoken word moves through an entire community like water,
like a river running its unstoppable course, subterranean at
times, re-emerging where geology permits it. In the same way
plays are performed: here tonight, gone tomorrow, starting in
Soweto, then disappearing, to surface again in New Brighton
or Langa or wherever, fostering a consciousness of solidarity
within a revolution already under way . . .

Examples from the USSR are so familiar that the briefest
summary of some of the more celebrated cases should
suffice.

There was Osip Mandelshtam who spent most of his time
in the 1930s either as a fugitive or in jail, where he was not
permitted to write: so he began to memorize his poems, or
to recite them to his wife Nadezhda for her to
memorize . . . and years afterwards, just before he died in
exile in a transit camp, they reconstructed everything they
had memorized and wrote it down, ensuring it would survive
in the minds of readers all over the world.

There was Boris Pasternak, untouchable even by Stalin
because of his great international reputation. But his friend
Olga Ivinskaya, vulnerable because they were not married,

could be jailed from 1949 to 1953, and again after Pasternak's death, from 1960 to 1964. (After which she published her own profoundly moving book to bear witness before the world.) He was allowed to write, but had to keep it to himself. *Novy mir* was prepared to publish a few extracts from *Doctor Zhivago*, but no more than that; and the only reason for their reluctance was that he had not portrayed the Revolution as a cake with a cherry on top. When at long last he had to accept that there was no legitimate form of making himself heard in Russian, he gave permission for his work to be published abroad. 'You have just invited me to attend my own execution,' he told the representative of Feltrinelli when negotiations were concluded in 1956: yet he preferred this to silence. And so he became a living example of Malraux's famous statement: 'Art does not submit. Art conquers.'

Pasternak's major disciple, Andrei Sinyavsky, was prosecuted together with Yuli Daniel, soon after the master's death. Ignoring all warnings, Sinyavsky refused to tone down his criticism of contemporaries who slavishly followed Stalin's directives. One result was that, when Stalinism came to its ignominious fall, tearing down with it the entire literary framework of reference of Party-oriented Social Realism, Sinyavsky retained his integrity as a writer. This in itself stimulated the increasing vehemence of his detractors; he became a thorn in the conscience of the Establishment. When he couldn't find anyone to print his stories in his own country he followed Pasternak's example and published abroad in the émigré journal *Kulturo* in Paris. In 1965 Sinyavsky and Daniel were arrested. For months the authorities tried to force an admission of 'deviance' from them (there was no other evidence against them), but they refused. Their trial in 1966 became a new chapter in the tortuous history of writers in an embattled situation, since even in the USSR no writer had previously been pilloried solely on the grounds of his fiction. Even this did not silence them: in his letters to his wife Sinyavsky continued to create a harrowing and moving image of life in jail; after his release these writings were published under the pseudonym Abram Tertz which Sinyavsky had used for his early publications abroad. A *Voice from the Chorus*, this 'silent bomb of a book' (in the words of Heinrich Böll), is one of the noblest literary documents of our time, based on Sinyavsky's most intimate thoughts and experiences in captivity: 'Man unconfined in space constantly aspires to go forward into the distance . . . But if he is constricted, cut down to size, reduced to the minimum, then his mind, deprived of forests and fields, creates an inner landscape out of its own innumerable resources.'

These words, like Sinyavsky's other winged phrase, 'Art is created in order to overcome death', also provide a motto to the life and work of Alexander Solzhenitsyn. He, too, could not be broken by imprisonment, humiliation, persecution or exile. When he was not allowed to write he would memorize, like Mandelshtam, thousands of lines to be written down years later. His entire career as a writer, in fact, began in jail, inspired and nourished by persecution; and in his own way, as Dostoievsky had done a century before, he learned to purify and enrich private experience and to turn it into a monument *against* violence, and *for* invincibility of compassion, the human being's capacity to endure.

But it is time to move on to other countries, other writers.

In the Philippines, where Marcos is reputed to keep a personal eye on the repression of writers, even whispering can be dangerous—and yet literature flourishes, as a commentator summarized it, 'in mimeographed papers, pamphlets, posters, secret discussion groups and propaganda by word of mouth'. In South Korea the world of letters is dominated by the figure of the heroic comedian Kim Chi Ha, jailed in 1970 for his satirical work, yet indomitable enough to smuggle out, right under the eyes of his guards, a volume of satirical ballads. Since 1975 he lives in solitary confinement, still fiercely committed to the belief that 'the way to achieve freedom and self-determination is the way of voluntary suffering.' In Egypt there is the lyrical poet Ahmed Fouad Negm, sent to prison in 1959 and smuggling out his first writings from there; after his release he met the blind singer Sheikh Imam, and now they spend their time either in jail or in hiding from the authorities, pouring forth their songs without interruption—as did Theodorakis when the colonels in Greece imprisoned him. And it would seem that, even though their songs are written in dialect, theirs are the only lyrics that have crossed all the frontiers of the Arab world, 'amateurishly recorded on cassette tapes,' writes Khalil Hindi, 'and smuggled from one country to another to be received by a wide audience of students, intellectuals and workers'.

Indonesia's leading writer is Pramoedya Ananta Toer, first imprisoned in the course of the struggle of liberation against the Dutch: aided by a few sympathetic Dutchmen he, too, smuggled out his work from prison. After independence he was released, only to land in trouble again with the Sukarno regime which seemed to have learned their trade from their erstwhile overlords. He was jailed on the Godforsaken island of Buru. Permission to write was granted him, provided he didn't use writing materials. So he, too, resorted to memorizing. He has now been in prison since 1965. During the past five years he has at least been allowed to write normally; and it is reported that he has already completed eight novels. In a recent interview in prison, when asked what his fourteen years of detention has meant to him, he answered in words which characterize the essential preoccupation of the writer: 'This has been a period of concentration to write better works.'

Harsh as it is, his fate still seems mild in comparison with what is happening in countries like the Argentine and Chile (South Africa's close allies and trusted friends), where thousands of people are murdered, while countless others are forced to flee, and where many leading writers and intellectuals simply 'disappear'. For them there is as little opportunity of continuing to write in jail as for those writers languishing in the prisons of Africa. (The Soyinkas and Awoonors can still count themselves 'lucky': at least they were released at some stage, and allowed to resume writing in exile—provided we never underestimate this *dur métier que l'exil!*—but this does not apply to Ngugi wa Thiongo in the liberal land of Kenya . . .) Yet even in these almost intolerable conditions the word of the writer has not been eclipsed.

Looking at Chile, one recalls the words of Jesus about the very stones crying out. For something quite unique has been happening there, beginning in Santiago, then spreading across the whole country: women—the most ordinary women, labourer women, washerwomen who can neither read nor write—have risen in protest against the silencing and the disappearance of their relatives and friends. They streamed to the textile factories where they begged for reject bits of cloth and wool. From this they make tapestries and appliqués which silently but spectacularly proclaim the simple terrible truths of their naked lives. Many of these pictures are in 'code'; many, it would seem, are direct and stark in their statements, but with a naïveté which seems to escape the scrutiny of the State machinery.

What do they hope to achieve with this? This was how one washerwoman replied to the question: 'We like to portray in our tapestries what people are living through, reality, things that say something. We have lived through much and we must explain it. We must find some way to say it.'

And another: 'I want people to know. Often one keeps silent through shame, but I'm going to tell these things; I'm not ashamed to do so because everything that has happened to me is true . . . I can't keep silent, because I have lived it.'

And a third: 'When all resources are exhausted, when misery knocks at the door, when hunger is the daily enemy, survival the only horizon . . . one must do something, act, refuse to give in. That's when we went to the factories to collect scraps of material. For everything, and humour too, has become a weapon in our struggle.'

In these conditions literature and art are forced back to their very roots, to elemental and rudimentary beginnings. Anything—but not silence. *I can't keep silent, because I have lived it.*

VII

It is time to round off our brief and very superficial excursion through history and geography. And what a depressing composite picture it seemed to show us of the writer never really 'at home' in the world. Sometimes his presence is tolerated; sometimes he is patronized; often all the weapons in the arsenal of the State are used against him: house arrest, detention, imprisonment, torture, exile, death.

Yet the final image to emerge from the palimpsest is that of the writer's ability to endure, and of the inability of all the organizations and instruments of Power irrevocably to silence the word uttered with so much integrity, humility and pride by the writer in a state of siege.

And what about us, in our situation in South Africa, threatened in so many ways and on so many levels? Neither history nor I can prescribe any solutions. The most we can do is to take note of some of the answers some of our predecessors and contemporaries have found—that is to say, once the writer, like Camus's rebel, has made the first essential choice between life and death, which in our situation implies the choice between writing and silence.

Having made this choice, a second presents itself: to leave the embattled society and write in exile, or to take the risk of continuing to work inside. This is a territory of experience where every individual has to decide for himself, and assume for himself the responsibilities of his choice. For Thomas

Mann or Brecht it was physically impossible to go on writing within the Third Reich; for Arthur Miller it was unthinkable to leave—even if, within the menaces of the McCarthy era, he had to resort to the codes of witch-hunting or an incident at Vichy to communicate what he so urgently had to say.

The writer who elects to stay in his society, has the option of allegory or of confrontation available to him. Post-war Poland, Czechoslovakia, Hungary and other countries have demonstrated the exhilarating possibilities of the allegorical or oblique method—but also, in some cases, the dangers inherent in it, notably that of obscurantism, where in order to get past the authorities the text becomes so cryptic as to lose much of its essential function of communication. On the other hand, the writer who chooses confrontation lives in constant peril, not only of having his work banned but of being persecuted in person. Even so, he has at his disposal several possibilities, including notably *tamishdat*, as Pasternak or Sinyavsky did; or semi-clandestine publication, as represented by the Hungarian *Profile*; or the final plunge of *zamishdat*.

It is my belief that we are fast approaching a situation in South Africa where *zamishdat* may be our only way out, and I must gravely warn the Government to beware of it, since in the end they will have to pay a greater price for it than writers. When the writers in a country are driven underground, it is an infallible sign of a crumbling which has already begun in society as a whole; in the long run no government can hope either to contain or to survive it. At the same time I must also sound a note of warning to writers: for *zamishdat* is not a fashionable, exciting little game but the ultimate recourse, in an extreme situation, of responsible people who have tried every other available option. And for the very reason that clandestinity can so easily offer protection to writers who are simply too bad to find a publisher anyway, we must make very sure indeed that, if our day of 'diving under' comes, we will make our choice only with the greatest circumspection and the most profound sense of responsibility. At the same time, should such a moment dawn, we dare not flinch from doing what we can no longer avoid.

It is my sincerest hope, even at this late stage, that the authorities who have already driven us to the edge, will stop in time to see the fatal folly of the course they have chosen: there still exists a small chance for them to save face. Unless they are prepared to change, they must stand warned that we shall go all the way, always at least one step ahead, in making sure that their lies are exposed, that reality is not distorted, that truth will prevail.

What our brief Cook's tour through history has demonstrated, is the infinite resourcefulness of the writer's mind in finding ways to make himself heard, discovering that from the very dangers which threaten his survival inspiration can be drawn, even if it means returning to the emblems woven and stitched by the washerwomen of Chile.

In the final analysis there is but one basic response a writer driven by his conscience can offer, which is both the simplest and the most difficult of all: and that is the response expressed in the *quality of his work*.

Even on the most practical level this is the only response effective in the long run: if Pasternak and Solzhenitsyn still burn in the conscience of the world, it is not only because they suffered and were persecuted, and not only because nothing could stop them from writing, but because of the quality of their work.

A lesser writer can disappear in the turmoil of the world. But if the work is worth it, it contains within itself the mechanisms that ensure its survival.

It contains, above all, the only mechanism really relevant to the writer's struggle in and with his world: great literature offers a guarantee against death. Even the writer working in the safest society imaginable must one day face this ultimate adversary, death. Our work, if it is good enough, is the only part of us which can survive the grave. This is the sole *raison d'être* for literature in a world which, otherwise, might easily sweep it aside. In the truth embedded in the writer's word lies that ineffable power feared so much by tyrants and tyrannies and other agents of death that they are prepared to stake everything they have against it. For they know only too well that no strategy or system can ever, finally, resist the word of truth.

I wish to acknowledge my debt to *Index on Censorship* from whose numbers many of my contemporary examples have been gleaned.

The Intellectual
and His World

(1980)

To say that the last quarter of the twentieth century presents us with a tough and practical world, with tough and practical demands on both society and the individual, is to state the obvious. Yet the obvious may require as much scrutiny as the cryptic or the arcane, since its very obviousness may tend to its being taken too much for granted. The result may be intellectual laziness and moral slackness. And this world of ours, provisionally described as tough and practical, demands above all a particular form of intellectual and moral courage—especially when it is approached from the perspective of the academic.

It has become customary to sneer at the impotence of the individual in general and the intellectual in particular. In a world overrun by masses and requiring, for its practical needs, ever-increasing common denominators, the individual appears a paltry and insignificant creature indeed, more often a hindrance than a help. And in a world demanding urgent solutions for problems like hunger, racism, exploitation, ideological and territorial expansionism, aggression and repression, the activity of the intellectual may appear not only futile but redundant, a luxury society can ill afford.

This is the context within which Lorca told his famous

anecdote about the rich man and his peasant neighbour taking a stroll through a particularly scenic landscape: the rich man stopped in ecstasy every few minutes to exclaim with genuine appreciation: 'How beautiful!' But all the poor man could do in response was to clutch his belly and repeat: 'I am hungry, I am hungry, I am hungry!' Again, this is the context within which one encounters the accusation: 'No book and no thought can stop a bullet from a gun!' Or: 'I was suffering, and you offered me a theory of relativity. I was oppressed, and you formed a Freedom and Justice Committee to debate the nature of oppression. I was put in jail and tortured by the Security Police, and you said liberty was a commendable thing.' It is the context within which a leading South African Sunday newspaper, reviewing the axing of staff and departments at a particular university, commented that this was only a logical and possibly even salutary step, in keeping with the practice in big business to eliminate non-profitable areas of production.

These arguments and accusations derive from a cartesian rigorism which divides thought and action into two separate categories divided by an either/or. In each group one finds throroughly well-meaning persons condemning what they regard as their opposite group: 'You are being merely intellectual . . . '/'You are being merely practical . . . ' There seems to be an unfortunate tendency in the West to think in these linear terms, these neat opposites. If you oppose the Government you are a communist; if you don't oppose it you're a fascist. And when an effort towards reconciliation is made, the solution usually seems to lie in creating a sliding scale containing thought on one end and action on the other, with the logical inference that the validity of thought lies in the measure in which it evolves into action, or prompts or promotes action. It seems to me an impoverishment of our experience to think in these terms. In fact, I would suggest that it is a line of thought which develops from either a misunderstanding or an obfuscation of the concepts 'thought' and 'action'; hence, of the concept 'intellectual'. It is the same sort of misunderstanding which, for such a long time, clouded the concepts of 'form' and 'content' in the arts.

Approached in one particular way one might suggest that 'thought' and 'action' are really two sides of the same coin, and that what matters is neither heads nor tails but the solid metal in between. In this context thought would be seen as interiorized action; action as expressive thought, or thought made visible. And neither can exist without the other: it is only in our impoverished interpretation of empirical processes that we fatefully separate them. But perhaps even the coin image is too mechanical: perhaps one should think in terms of an iceberg, with nine-tenths of thought submerged in order to allow one-tenth of action to protrude.

Although this may be a truer image, we are left with the situation I outlined at the beginning of my talk, in terms of which certain *kinds* of action seem to be preferable to others: preferable, at least, within the frameworks of the 'practical' demands of organized society. We are left, in other words, with the hungry man who cannot be fed on beauty; the jailed prisoner who cannot be freed through noble dictums; the company that cuts staff in order to 'rationalize' and which demands the same of universities. But in this situation, too, it seems to me that an either/or approach defeats the purpose and is too easy a way out. No one disputes that a hungry man should be fed, an unjustly imprisoned man freed, or an ailing company be made profitable. But having fulfilled all these obligations, would society then be a more just and free place to live in? Would people automatically be more fulfilled or the much vaunted 'quality of life' be enhanced *sans plus*? Put in the simplest possible terms: can man really live by bread alone? To take it one step further, remaining within the framework of our set examples: if Lorca's hungry man is given his daily bread, can one deny his well-fed neighbour his delight in something beautiful? Can a climate for justice, in

which the unjustly jailed are set free, be created without the
dedicated activity of those who insist on the basic
requirement of justice in society? And once our company has
been made profitable, is there not another set of rules to
measure the 'profitability' of an institution for higher
education? Balanced books are a good and honourable thing,
but these do not rule out other kinds of books which create a
balanced mind. 'Bread for one yen' says the Japanese
proverb, 'For the other yen, white hyacinths.'

And so we are really back where we started: 'the intellectual
and his world'. It may seem that we are now entitled to ask:
What is the function of the intellectual in his world? But in
Hamlet's words: *Madam, I know not 'seems'*. For it is, indeed, as
unseemly a question as was the suggested dichotomy
between 'thought' and 'action'. To pose this question would,
after all, be to revive the dichotomy I have tried to discredit: it
would imply a difference between an 'intellectual' and, say,
an 'ordinary man', whatever either of these terms may mean.
When I was caught up in the student protests in Paris in 1968
there was one particular march in which a million people
took part, just after Daniel Cohn Bendit had been expelled
from France, and a million voices shouted: 'We are all
German Jews'—probably the only occasion in history when
the French showed any liking for the Germans. But
obviously nobody was so ridiculous as to take this in its literal
sense. A form of poetry was on the streets that day; and a
million people affirmed their common humanity and their
common opposition to a system of laws and a pattern of
society which denied or threatened that humanity. In this
sense, we are all either 'ordinary men' or 'intellectuals'—or
both: even though, in Orwell's immortal term, some may be
more equal than others.

All I am trying to clarify is that asking about the function of
the intellectual may be posing the wrong question. Let us
rather, more cautiously, enquire about the function of that

part in each one of us which is involved with intellectual activity: an enquiry which obviously has particular relevance within the framework of a university. For however 'modern' or 'practical' or 'pragmatic' or 'society-oriented' we may have become, I should still like to see, glimmering through the gloom, something of the original 'universality' in the word 'university': and if, as an institution, it is also becoming, through need and necessity, a career-orientated machine, it cannot ever, without denying itself, shed its function of shaping, broadening, stimulating and directing intellectual enquiry as the submerged nine-tenths of its unwieldy iceberg.

In thus directing my brief exploration towards the 'intellectual' half or nine-tenths of 'universal man', I accept, with Sir Herbert Read, that 'I am not concerned with the practicability of a programme. I am only concerned to establish the truth.' This is an ambitious activity into which one can enter only as an individual: thought is as exclusive to the individual as birth or death; and, I should like to think, as definitive. It is only natural that this activity of the individual should more often than not find itself in conflict with the accepted patterns of society: it is within this context that teaching has, rightly I think, been termed 'a subversive activity'. For in that territory of the mind where man is utterly and adventurously alone—even though he may assume responsibility for all men in what he undertakes (just as Sir Edmund Hilary, in a sense, climbed Everest for all mankind) the individual, putting everything at stake, can be guided only by the full and overwhelming reality of *that situation*, and not by general rules or by tradition. It is a religious solitude which can lead to perdition or redemption: but precisely because the stakes are so high it is an adventure unequalled by any other. To speak once again with Read:

'Life depends on the agitation set up by a few eccentric individuals. For the sake of that life, that vitality, a community must take certain risks, must admit a modicum of

200

heresy. It must live dangerously if it would live at all.'

Or elsewhere:

'I realize that form, pattern, and order are essential aspects of existence; but in themselves they are the attributes of death. To make life, to ensure progress, to create interest and vividness, it is necessary to break down form, to distort pattern, to change the nature of our civilization.'

This seems a lofty and confused ideal. But it is possible to be more specific. I have no intention to be exhaustive in suggesting a few possibilities of intellectual action: only to venture a couple of yards across the border of this 'undiscover'd country' which differs from Hamlet's in that its travellers do survive to tell the tale.

'We must grasp what grips us,' said the literary theoretician Emil Staiger: a concept which may be broadened to intellectual activity as a whole. It is surely not part of our human condition simply to endure what happens: even in circumstances where it would appear impossible actively to influence the course of events the simple but momentous act of clarification—of establishing *what* is happening, and *why*—may become the starting point of significant social action. It works in two stages: informing oneself; and transmitting that information to others. The entire momentum of social action against authoritarian silence or authoritarian lies begins with the establishment of these two series of facts: what is happening; and why. No authority should be allowed to create a set of circumstances within which it becomes possible for anyone to say: *I didn't know*. What seems a very simple, basic procedure may, in societies like our own, prove to be an act of courage. It was the starting point of the Fischers and Mandelas in a struggle for a modicum of sanity in an insane structure. (Had the challenge of their intellectual enquiry been met instead of thwarted, violence could have been avoided.) It was the principle to which Beyers Naudé and the Christian Institute dedicated themselves. The Black Consciousness Movement, the

201

Students' Council of Soweto, *The World*, Steve Biko, Donald Woods, and a fair percentage of the thousands of books banned in this country have been silenced in their various ways for this same basic reason: that truth is unbearable in a society which is built upon the lie. And only through the action of dedicated individuals, through the unflinching moral and intellectual enquiry of an independent mind, can silence and the lie be countered. We have an elemental need to know what grips us.

This enquiry is not directed exclusively towards a world of so-called external or social fact. The courage of the mind, which implies in our time Tillich's 'courage to be', demands also an enquiry of its own processes: of language, and of thought itself. We all know, when dealing with an estate agent, that 'charming' really means 'bloody awful', 'functional' means 'falling to pieces', and 'interesting view' means an unrestricted view of your neighbour's fence. But we also have to probe the language of authoritarianism: we have followed the semantic metamorphosis of 'apartheid' into 'separate development' into 'parallel development' into 'equal opportunity' into 'constellation of states'; of BOSS into DONS (a curious upgrading which the Mafia would appreciate), etc. But these are only the more glaring, obtrusive examples; and in an authoritarian society semantics is a very subtle game. We need only look at words like 'state security', 'law and order' and others to become aware of it. Among other processes one should be wary of the process of *definition*: our own society reveals startling similarities with that of Stalinist Russia described thus by Roland Barthes:

> In the Stalinist world, in which *definition*, that is to say the separation of Good and Evil, becomes the sole content of language, there are no more words without values attached to them, so that finally the function of writing is to cut out one stage of a process: there is no

more lapse of time between naming and judging, and the closed character of language is perfected.

The search for truth, which is the search of the individual's intellectual activity, implies also an attack on facile polarities. In our dangerous society almost everything is experienced in terms of either/or. The most glaring: black/white; segregation/integration, etc . . . . In such a closed situation, I suggest, intellectual activity can contribute to a defusing of the tension created by simplistic polarities by clarifying the complexity of the issues involved and by exploring other options.

In immediate, practical terms: several previously white-dominated societies on our borders have in recent years and even months demonstrated a variety of different options. On a limited scale it applies even to Namibia, where some white Afrikaners have scrapped laws and rules regarded by other white Afrikaners as guarantees of national identity. If Namibia can survive without pass laws, group areas or the relevant sections of the Immorality Act, why should we be the only country in the world to need them for our survival?

South Africa has entered an exciting period in which, for the first time in thirty years, a limited range of new possibilities is being debated and in which the word 'change' is no longer, in itself, anathema. Intellectual integrity would lie neither in summarily dismissing it nor in accepting it as sufficient in itself. Instead, the true adventure of the mind would ensure that the range of possibilities be expanded immeasurably both in width and in depth, and that not only matters of bread and of physical survival be explored but also, and above all, those matters of intellect and morality without which it would be presumptuous to claim for ourselves the name of *man*. Without quantity we may not be able to survive: without quality it would not be worth while to.

Writing Against Silence

(1980)

It is a great honour indeed to be associated, through this prize, with the name of that great champion of justice, liberty and the common humanity of all people, Martin Luther King. His name has a particular significance within the context of South Africa, in which one cannot fail to recognize many of the ingredients of the society within which Martin Luther King himself operated, and which finally brought about the violent death of an eminently non-violent man. Through this award contact is established, across the barriers of time and space, and across the barrier which separates life from death, between people of different times and countries; and the experience of one is revalidated in terms of the experience of another.

In A *Dry White Season* I have tried to accept that responsibility one owes to one's society and one's time; it was conceived in anguish and written in pain and in rage, but not in hate. Even when one's conscience drives one to a position of *J'accuse*, it can be valid as a literary experience only if it derives not from the sterility of a merely negative attitude but from an all-consuming belief that man *can* be rescued from his blindness and his follies; and that the world *can* be a more just and a more free place to live in than it is. If one is driven to say 'No' it should transcend the immediacy of denial to become an affirmation of something more just, more true, and more compassionate than whatever one has been allowed to experience in the past.

Perhaps the very phrase 'allowed to' suggests a key to the situation: in any authoritarian society, of which South Africa is but one example, there is a very narrowly defined, circumscribed area of experience 'allowed' to the individual. The 'safety of the state'—the phrase usually invoked, also when *A Dry White Season* was initially banned—determines the freedom 'allowed' the individual. In these circumstances the act of writing becomes an act of defiance, inasmuch as it challenges the absolute right of an authority either to prescribe or to proscribe the creative processes. Writing is an affirmation, not only of the individual, but, through him, of the nameless and voiceless multitude who must rely on him to define the validity of their right to be.

I am often asked, and sometimes reproached in the process, how it is possible to resort to writing novels in a situation like the South African, where the realities of suffering and frustration are so overwhelming in their immediacy. The implication is, of course, that writing is an escape, an opting out, from a situation which seems to require actions rather than words. But I should like to suggest, as I have done so often in the past, that, especially in a situation like the one in South Africa, the written word in itself can assume the weight of significant action. If this were not so, why would authoritarian regimes resort to censorship? Why would governments feel so particularly and peculiarly threatened by the published word?

In South Africa censorship forms only part of a large and complicated machinery of repression. And this machinery is itself but a symptom of a deeper sickness, a sickness of the mind; it is a symptom of a psychosis of fear which derives, in a diabolically logical way, from the simple fact that people are kept apart and denied the opportunities of getting to know one another. It is this separateness, this terrible apartheid that goes far beyond the dimensions of politics which to me formed the starting point of A *Dry White Season*. And the cruelties of the surface, however horrifying they may be in their own right, are only signs of that deeper cruelty which denies people the right to put out a hand and touch a fellow man: which, I think, is the ultimate symbolic gesture in the life and thought of Martin Luther King.

Writing about this, exploring it, probing it, trying to get to the roots of it, becomes an act of challenging and resisting the entire existence of such a system. The cover-up can only be countered with exposure, the lie with truth, silence—including the silence of a people who have given up asking questions about their own condition—with the word. One function of the writer in a restricted society, I believe very firmly, lies in simply revealing to people *what is happening*: what they themselves allow to happen. Writing is one of the surest responses to the Nuremberg plea of ignorance: provided it goes beyond the surface of appearances and facts—these being the domain of the politician, the sociologist, the historian. What matters to the writer is the human dimension: not ideologies or symptomatic remedies, but the reality of people suffering and living. He is not a provider of ready answers, but an asker of questions.

In this respect I should like to see the Martin Luther King Memorial Prize not simply as an award to A *Dry White Season*, but as an acknowledgement of the indispensable work done by writers in South Africa: and a major part of this writing is done by black writers, most of them young, most of them persecuted, many of them silenced very soon. I am thinking, especially, of the writers of Soweto; the writers of the magazine *Staffrider*, who deserve the interest, the encouragement and the support of an international community. community.

They are not writing in a void; and they are not writing in vain. Already, in the last year, there have been signs of at least a possibility of change in South Africa, something which had been unthinkable in the Vorster and earlier eras. So far much of this new movement exists purely on the level of words and vague promises; and unless these are soon translated into effective and profound action, the frustrated hopes of the majority of South Africans may result in a volcanic explosion compared to which Soweto in 1976 may appear like a celebration of Guy Fawkes.

However, I have a measure of cautious hope that Martin Luther King's way—the way of non-violent transition to a more just, non-racist society—has not yet been entirely closed. And writing, I firmly believe, is one way of keeping it open.

The Freedom to Publish

(1980)

I

Freedom as such, hence also the freedom to publish, is immeasurable, as a current of water, or the wind, is immeasurable, perhaps even imperceptible, unless judged in relation to something else, or unless its progress is interrupted, intercepted or threatened by an obstacle. Freedom becomes measurable, significant and important to the extent in which unfreedom exists and hampers it. In other words, our consciousness of freedom implies the existence of unfreedom.

Freedom is never an absolute, a Promised Land to be entered and to be lived in. It can be perceived only in the act of transcending unfreedom.

Unfreedom is our condition, freedom is our desire: in between lies our nature, in which lies embedded the urge to transcend limits, frontiers, restrictions, barriers.

Within this framework, the act of writing, and its corollary, the act of publishing, becomes a significant statement about the desire for freedom, which is part of the urge to live. To write and to publish define and demonstrate man's need to transcend the limits of his unfreedom. Approached in this way, it is not a luxury but a prerequisite for a significant

208

existence; not the kind of privilege that may be bestowed, wearily or warily, by a benign authority, on the 'deserving', i.e. the subservient, but a basic need.

This need forms part of man's complex need to communicate, an extension of a biological urge without which even animals can hardly survive; and which, in man, has evolved to a state in which his very humanity is at stake. Speaking as a writer among publishers, I should suggest that this urgent act of communication can be approached from two ends.

II

In the first place, it may be approached from the end of the writer, the initial transmitter of the complex cultural codes signified by his poem, or play, or novel. In the process of shaping his work and giving it being—drawing on all his inner resources and on the totality of his experience, both as an individual and as a factor involved in and committed to mankind—the writer experiences two distinct stages.

The first is entirely and intensely personal, one of the most private experiences imaginable: this is the process of writing as such, which is an act of formulating and shaping experience in order to give it a name. And this in itself is only a symptom of the deeper and more urgent process involved, namely the search to attain a grasp on the self, to define it, and, in the process, to change and enlarge it. Without this stage the search for truth embodied in the act of writing cannot be initiated, because essentially the writer can only be true to himself, to his experience, to that glimpse of truth accessible to him in terms of his temperament, inclination and life. But, taken one step further, it becomes truth to that in him which makes him part of the common body of humanity.

Even the privacy of this process can be invaded or

threatened—as happened to me when Security Police searched my house, perused all my notes for a novel, even confiscated my typewriters; as happens to many of my black colleagues in South Africa when, sometimes simply on the strength of having written one poem or one play, they are detained for an indeterminate period, or intimidated in a variety of ways in order to dissuade them from embarking on their search for truth. (In one instance a friend of mine, because he is black, is not allowed to travel—not even inside South Africa—which effectively keeps him away from a region where he has situated his novel in progress and which he has to revisit in order to check his topographical and other facts.)

Yet, however vitally important this phase of writing may be, it is only the starting point in the process of communication. Once the exploration has been undertaken, once the statement has been encoded in writing, it has to be published, 'made public', in order to test its relevance within the context of communal life, and in order for that grain of truth to survive and prevail in the world. The wholly private truth has its value for the individual concerned, but it brings no enlightenment to man. It *has* to be private and individual to start with; but to become valid it must transcend the life of the individual.

Because of the intensity of the communication involved a certain resemblance with the sexual act becomes inevitable: the writing as such offers an important release and a discovery of self, which suggests masturbation or some form of coitus interruptus; through publication the process is completed, the other is reached, a situation of give-and-take is established, metaphysical osmosis takes place, as in complete intercourse.

At this point the alliance between writer and publisher becomes decisive: not, or not only, as partners in business, each indispensable to the other, but as allies in a vital process of communication; that is why, almost invariably, the relationship between writer and publisher becomes such a precious, multi-faceted and many-layered experience. Together, they liberate a peculiar perception of truth and offer it a lease of life among men.

In a society where human dignity is respected, this function of public-action of the private truth is held sacred. Whenever a society deviates from the ways of truth—for reasons of self-interest, 'state security', accumulation of wealth or power or whatever—it feels insecure in the face of publication and takes steps to inhibit this vital process in order artificially and violently to survive itself. The truth is dangerous to the lie; the word poses a threat to silence. Hence, literature, and publication, are regarded as enemies, terrorists, saboteurs within a closed or corrupt society which celebrates and perpetuates the lie: not because they are, in themselves, instruments of terror but because the closed society cannot bear the truth.

This places an imperative on writer and publisher to carry on their dangerous business, *most particularly* in those societies where they are threatened: the very existence of the threat defines the need for truth, i.e. the need for publication.

III

But I suggested in the beginning that the subject could also be approached from the opposite end, i.e. the end of the reader. And it seems to me that the reader, who is the real loser in a state of censorship or oppression, is too often disregarded in an enquiry of this nature.

In terms of literature itself, the work exists only as a given potential, a spectrum of possibilities, a latent electric current temporarily stored. In order to fulfil its potential, realize its possibilities, release the current, it has to be 'switched on' by the reader. The reader is to the book what the conductor and the orchestra are to the score of a symphony: he is the 'performing artist' who brings to life what has been enclosed, dormant, in the book. In writing his work the author has literally put his whole life at stake for the mere possibility, or in the mere hope, of finding his grain of truth. Now, in a real sense—and often without himself being aware of it—the reader puts at stake *his* whole life, *his* personality, *his* experience in entering into this literary semblance of the sexual act. The one-night stand is possible in reading as it is in sex: but the full potential of communication is experienced only when the fullness of two lives and two personalities offer themselves to each other in the act, totally exposed, totally vulnerable, wholly themselves—in a fulfilment which may create a new life undreamt of before.

In more pragmatic terms, involving notably the socio-political, the reader, as citizen of a state, has an inalienable right of access to truth: it is, in the final analysis, as imperative as the access to food and drink and shelter, since man does not live by either bread or politics alone. The published word—i.e. a view of truth made public—offers one of the most important safeguards against the lie; or, seen positively, one of the most important gateways to truth. Now, truth has this peculiar attribute of having to exist both privately and collectively: starting out as the private discovery of the individual writer, it is made public in order to be appropriated by other individuals, each in terms of his own experience and awareness. But the authoritarian organization involved in ordering the public existence of an entire community must, by its very nature, think and act and legislate in terms of common denominators, collectivities, and masses: the alienation of the individual becomes inevitable. And a book offers a way out by publicly offering access to a privately perceived truth. In this way the lie, which thrives on collectivity and whose guarantee is the common denominator, can be countered.

This means that if a reader is denied access to a book *his*

212

freedom is jeopardized, *his* chances of glimpsing the truth are diminished, *his* right to know and to discover is denied. In this way the sanity and the fullness of life of the community as a whole are threatened when the freedom to publish is inhibited. Both private and communal life become geared to distortion, silence, or lies masked as 'official truths'. And once again an imperative is imposed on writer, publisher and reader alike to ensure that access to the truth is not blocked.

IV

It follows from what I have said that censorship, the most spectacular threat to the freedom to publish, is invariably a political act, not a moral or religious one; and it derives from the urge of power to protect itself, to perpetuate itself, to prevail.

And probably because its origins are so sinister, its workings also tend to be obscure. Speaking from within my experience in South Africa, which has one of the most draconian censorship systems in the so-called 'free world', the most pernicious effects of censorship are not caused by the actual prohibition of books—although that, God knows, is bad enough (among other things it has wiped out an entire generation of black writers in the 1960s and is threatening to do so again at the moment): the most iniquitous results are those created by the climate of fear, suspicion and uncertainty *surrounding* the actual machinations of an Act of Parliament. Printers become scared to print since they may lose lucrative contracts from pressure-groups if they print works of a certain nature or by certain authors (I have experienced this personally); booksellers become scared to stock titles which run the risk of being banned (I have experience of this too); publishers become scared to publish because they may be victimized, or because they may lose large amounts of money, or because their own future may be jeopardized (sadly, I have experience of this as well); and, in the last instance, writers may become scared to write (I trust that I shall never become an example of this).

But for the writer there are ways out, through *zamishdat* or any of the multitude of ways devised by ingenious people in our own age and before us. The problem is that these devious ways threaten the stimulating relationship between writer and publisher, which can be creative in both directions.

It is in this spirit, and for these reasons, that in conclusion, as a writer who has suffered the full violence of the frontal attacks of a system of censorship devised by a racist regime, I appeal to the publishers of the world: help the writer, stand by him, offer him that solidarity which will guarantee the survival of the word of truth in this dangerous and difficult world.

Imagining the Real

(1981)

I

Man's access to truth has never been direct or easy. Stumbling through the minefield of modern and not-so-modern theories on the nature and meaning of myth, I find in this proposition the clue most relevant to my personal convictions and experience as a writer. For whatever else myth may have been in its successive stages (ranging from primitive ritual and probably pre-verbal experience, through the eloquent phases of ancient Egypt, Greece, Rome and Scandinavia to the psychologies of Freud and Jung, and the anthropologies and semiotics of Lévi-Strauss and Barthes), what appears to me its most valid aspect in the modern literary context, is its ceaseless efforts to transcend the mere *facts* of things in order to arrive at what may be termed their *truth*. Or in another terminology: to progress from *meaning* to *significance*. By enquiring into the how, why and wherefore of existence, myth tries to explain not only why *this* region is so barren of vegetation, or why *these* two trees have their branches so inextricably intertwined, or why the hare has a split upper lip, but why the world is what it is; and what the place of man is within it. By occupying itself with the universals of the human condition, it bestows a sense upon

215

what Buddhists would call the *suchness* of things. In its original form and function it is the essence of religious experience: word made flesh; flesh made word.

In short, myth transcends the word just as, in another sense, it anticipates the word. The word is the meeting-place of pre- and post-, of before and after, as in the falling of a stone is gathered the silence preceding it and that following it. And this gathering function is, as I see it, quintessential to the concept of myth: there is no distance between the narrator, the myth and the listener. In the experience of telling it, consubstantiation is effected. And it is through this experience that man is not only *taught* about the world, which would be the province of philosophy or didactics, but *integrated* with the world: in acknowledging the unity of personal experience—no, more: of human experience— myth restores man to his 'place' within the world, neither as mere observer nor as victim, but as creative participant.

II

If this is the true sense and function of myth, it would seem, certainly at first glance, as if ours is essentially a non-mythical, even an anti-mythical, age. It is not merely indifferent to or ignorant about myth, but aggressively against it: even on the most mundane level the pseudo-scientific function of myth in primitive, homogeneous, religiously oriented society has been superseded by the verifiable explorations of natural science in a sophisticated, heterogeneous, secular society. Fact has become the enemy of myth. And as Thomas Love Peacock expressed it a century ago in his novel *Gryll Grange*: 'there can be . . . no Naiad in a stream that turns a cotton-mill; no Oread in a mountain dell, where a railway train deposits a cargo of Vandals; no Nereids or Oceanitides along the seashore, where a coastguard is watching for smugglers.' No wonder that Marx concluded, as K. K. Ruthven notes in his brief introductory study on *Myth*, that 'imaginative creations are made redundant by technological innovations.' In those instances where the twentieth century has created the illusion of its own myths, they have been manipulated by politicians into the antithesis of the primeval ritualistic explorations of creation, the awakening of spring, and the cycle of life: from the German myth of racial supremacy, of which South Africa is offering a contemporary mutation, is derived not life, but death and destruction.

Our epoch seems by its very nature to exclude the possibility of myth: it is secular, not inspired by or aspiring to religion; it is divisive, not cohesive; the very virtues which have contributed towards shaping it—democracy, individualism, concern for the exploited—have been distorted into the vices of vulgarity, mediocrity and new forms of tyranny and exploitation. In this context the tediously repetitive yet perpetually unconvincing obituary of the novel has, in itself, become characteristic of the age.

III

But perhaps this very phenomenon should provide a clue to the stubborn survival of myth. The constant proclamation of the death of the novel, the redundancy of poetry, the irrelevance of literature in solving the pressing problems of the world (famine, oppression, injustice, the systematized lie) should be seen in perspective—and the note of wishful thinking, born from distress and more than just a touch of panic, should not be missed. Literature angers the advocates of the brave new world precisely because they fear the harm it can do to their devastatingly logical systems and tyrannies: that is, because it has some mysterious power in a world that would like to pretend an evolution beyond the need for mystery.

217

And this power is, I should suggest, the residual magic of myth. Literature in our world fulfils what it can of the function of myth in a seemingly more simple society.

Notably since Joyce's *Ulysses* the employment of ancient myths in modern guise has become one of the most characteristic narrative techniques of the twentieth century, to the point where it often degenerates into what one American critic has called mere 'myth-mongering'. Yet where it *succeeds* it becomes not only an exciting device creating different levels of meaning or experience within narrative, but a disturbing and profoundly valid way of restating old truths within the context of changed and changing times. It is, after all, not only the parallels between Leopold Bloom and Ulysses which are meaningful in Joyce's novel, but the discrepancies—as a dramatic illustration, among many other things, of the diminishing stature of the hero in our time. In the work of the Afrikaans novelist Etienne Leroux myth is invariably the point of departure: and if the ancient Cybelian mysteries surrounding the death and rebirth of Attis are reduced, in one of his novels, to an advertising campaign promoting the sale of plastic blinds; or the seven days of creation and man's exposure to Good and Evil are grotesquely parodied in the initiation of a goy into a Jewish household, it is Leroux's way of insisting that man cannot live without myth: we continue to perform the same rituals and functions even if the gestures have lost their original meaning . . . and even if the death of myth in itself becomes the sustaining myth of our time. To Leroux myth is the awareness of the numinous, the glimpse of the beyond, the perception of significance without which life is inconceivable. In the green infancy of humanity people lived among myths, enveloped by myths: today, in our writing, we go *in search of* myth, of what shards of it remain in a broken world.

In a recent *Time* essay (15 December 1980) Lance Morrow spoke about 'the endless rediscovery of the wheel': without rediscovering and restating the obvious, he argues, the essential symbols and beliefs by which we survive may decline and disappear: 'The business of forgetfulness and rediscovery,' says Morrow, 'may be part of a vast dialectic sifting and refinement by which history discovers, and interminably rediscovers, whatever is worth keeping.'

In this lies the deepest sense of the 'return to myth' in so many novels and plays of our time. But what such works achieve in an overt, sometimes over-emphatic and deliberately spectacular, manner, is really what *all* important literature does all the time: rediscovering the wheel, reviving the abiding truths which determine the relationships among men and between man and the world. It is of little value simply to state certain truths: without living and experiencing them, they remain if not invalid at least inactive. *Life must be lived in order to be understood.* And literature, when it functions as myth, i.e. when it is most true to itself, achieves this by immersing the reader in a variety of experiences he may otherwise have missed. Vicarious experience it may be, but none the less profound—for several reasons, of which I suggest only a few.

It has become a cliché that most of us live in a state of alienation—whether one sees it in the Marxist or the Sartrean and Camusian sense, whether in the social, the political, the philosophical, the ethical, the religious or any other dimension. An essential element of this alienation is that mass societies obviate the need for the individual to think, feel or decide for himself. But the solitary act of choice which lies at the root of the reading experience exerts a double influence on the individual: first he is taken out of himself by entering into the new world of what he is reading; and eventually he is restored to himself and to his world, enriched by what he has drawn from that experience. He has glimpsed the possibility of a new significance in the world he inhabits. It is the individual's perception of the possibility of a truth larger than himself.

After all, in an age of intense specialization more and more specialists know more and more about less and less: which is another cliché. (And as clichés are a starting point of myth, it is not without reason that I constantly fall back on them.) The 'ordinary person' is more and more bewildered not only by the *variety*, but by the sheer bulk of information flooding over him. Each specialist claims an exclusive access to a specific territory, however small: with the result that the mathematician knows next to nothing about microbiology, and the botanist just as little about astrology—and the 'ordinary man' almost nothing of nothing, because disciplines become more and more isolated. (Even 'literary experts' are trying their damnedest to draw literature into a similar watertight enclave accessible only to them.) Literature, having replaced myth in the modern world, is one of the few remaining domains within which the individual can still obtain a view of life as a whole: hence the unity of individual experience and the unity of human experience I have referred to earlier. The literary myth both restores and guarantees this complex and enriching unity.

II

But is this not illusion? Is it not, as many scientifically minded people would have it, an *escape from reality*, and as such more pernicious than ennobling?

Most emphatically NOT!

What Chesterton said in a slightly different context, may, in ours, be applied in an even more revealing sense to myth and hence to literature-as-myth: 'Fairy tales make rivers run with wine only to make us remember, for one wild moment, that they run with water.'

This is what I had in mind when I suggested that literature does not only draw the reader away from his familiar world, but also, if it is successful as literature, restores him, enriched, to his own.

What is basically required, and what is offered by literature functioning as myth in a bewildering and secular age, is to *imagine the real*. Not to avoid what *is*, by offering a substitute or a palliative, but to experience what exists so intensely that through the imagination it realizes its full potential. Just as Proustian memory not only recaptures the lost and forgotten moment but makes it more vivid than it had initially been, so imagination brings reality into its own: only through rivers running with wine do we really perceive, as if for the first time, the running waters of the time we live in. It is an act and an experience which restores that mythical significance to life without which it would simply flow through us, unobstructed and unperceived. Myth in literature creates the obstacle through which we recognize and acknowledge the existence both of ourselves and the world. This is the difficult and indirect access to truth I have suggested at the outset of my paper.

V

In this essential respect, then, literature, when it is true to its primitive function, can never be other than a quest for truth, through an imagining of the real. And I should like to conclude these introductory remarks in the terms of a myth of the Khoisan peoples of Southern Africa, as immortalized by both Olive Schreiner and Laurens Van der Post:

In this myth, a young hunter, thirsty from wandering through the bush, stops at a pool and bends over to drink. In his stooped position he suddenly glimpses the reflection of a great white bird in the water, the most beautiful creature he has ever seen in his life. When he looks up, the bird has disappeared from the sky; but having seen that brilliant reflection he knows it exists. And from that moment he spends the rest of his life in search of the great white bird. Many years pass; and at last, when he is very old and close to death, he is directed to a high and perpendicular cliff rumoured to be the home of the white bird of truth. It appears unscalable; yet mustering his last strength he starts climbing. For days on end he struggles up the sheer face of the cliff until, too weak to continue, he sinks down on a narrow ridge where he lies staring up, through breaking eyes, at the forever unreachable summit. And suddenly a single white feather comes fluttering down and lands on his breast before he dies.

I know of no more moving symbol of the quest of the writer who, through the imagination, makes the real more vibrantly real than before, and deepens fact into mythical truth.

The Languages of Culture

(1982)

I

Culture can be defined so narrowly ('the Great Masterpieces of philosophy, the arts, and science'), or so widely ('all the distinctive spiritual and material, intellectual and emotional features characterizing a society') as to be almost meaningless. Yet we are all aware not only of its existence but of the precariousness of its existence; aware not only of the need to foster it and to include it in our projections for the future of humanity, but of the paradox inherent in this aim—since conscious 'protection' and 'encouragement', by governments or the large organs and organizations of society, often brings about the opposite effect and instead of liberating individuals and nations merely succeeds in enslaving them by shaping them to preconceived moulds. Almost inevitably, a 'cultural programme' forms part of the grand design of any totalitarian regime; by controlling the creation of art, the structures of education, the scope of ethics, the direction and application of scientific and religious enquiry, even the well-intentioned government or its extensions may inhibit culture rather than stimulate it. The most one can hope for is to help, as circumspectly as possible, to encourage, or simply to *allow*, the conditions and climate within which culture can come into its own.

223

II

It may be useful to define this 'own' by thinking of culture, not as a content or a series or cluster of contents, but most especially as a constantly developing cluster of structures. And even this should be defined more specifically. What we are confronted with in culture, is not an expanding, yet finite, set of 'things', of 'events', of 'actions', of 'products', or 'processes'—but with things, events, actions, products and processes which, through their interrelationships, *produce meaning*. This, to me, is the distinguishing mark of culture: it is that territory or dimension of existence in which meaning emerges; more precisely, that experience of meaning in which the individual is creatively related to the collective.

It follows that meaning, approached in this manner, can never be merely affirmative, but must inevitably be open-ended towards whatever lies beyond. Culture does not endorse or condone: it emerges constantly into meanings more fully articulated than those that went before. It is akin to language. More: it is a language, a set of languages, in its own right.

In order to articulate, it must proceed from a context, a (resilient, expanding) framework of reference within which the private and the public can meet and communicate. Which explains why the glorious periods of 'high culture' in human history—the Athens of Pericles, the Florence of the Medici, the Spain of the Moors, Elizabethan England . . .— almost invariably turned out to be those in which the 'culturally active', the 'meaning-producing' segment of society shared a system of values and references (at the expense of a deprived, exploited and suppressed minority— or, sometimes, majority?)

For many centuries, in the West, the nature of this context was determined by Christianity: not, as Eliot would have it, because religion necessarily informs culture, but simply because Christianity as a system determined the 'shape of

224

thought' in the West. But the hegemony of Christianity has been shattered in the course of the last century; and in opposition to it Marxism has emerged as the motivating factor in the creation of meaning in society. These two, the one religious, the other secular, share a utopian view of the world. And however much they may differ in most respects, at least the origins of both reveal strikingly similar precepts.

The violent reaction of Christianity to Marxism, it seems to me, derives not only from the fact that the former, itself unable to 'deliver the goods', sees in the utopian vision of Marxism a secular threat to itself, but from something more subtle: in the *collapse* of Marxism (evident in many ways, and in many parts of the world) Christianity sees, more devastatingly than in its earlier triumphs, *the confirmation of its own failure*. We are living amid the ruins of not one, but two, utopian visions of the world: two cohesive spiritual empires which may have enslaved humanity in many respects but also set it free to dream. Within both great systems culture could flourish ('up to a point', of course, until the rot set in); both inspired the production of meaning by providing the conditions in which languages of culture could evolve ('up to . . . '). Now we live within the void left by the crumbling of the large frameworks. We may be more exposed to the 'world at large' than ever before in the history of humanity; the globe has shrunk to the size of an airport, time to the length of a radio wave—and yet there is less 'universality' than before, since we have lost the referential systems within which *meaning* could be produced.

In his wonderful sequence of essays *In Bluebeard's Castle* (offered as 'Some Notes Toward the Re-definition of Culture') George Steiner has dwelt upon the devaluation of language as a valid system of cultural communication; in its place, he suggests, music may be establishing itself as the new metalanguage. Yet it seems to me that music operates in two main ways, both directed either away from or against culture as an experience of the production of meaning: either it drives individuals out of their social milieu into the privacy of the study or drawing-room, where records can be indulged in—oh, beautifully—in total privacy; or, in the discos and festivals of the young, where music is offered as 'total communication'; it actually functions as a *substitute* for meaning; it may even—like advertising, like the mass media—cover up for the *absence* of meaning. And the dizzy succession of top pops would seem to confirm this impression. Culture is more than 'doing things together'; more than 'dancing to the same beat'—which is what seaweed, too, does as the tides come in and recede.

In this vacuum, this absence of a creative context for the production of meaning, one might find some indicators indispensable for the sort of enquiry UNESCO has embarked on.

III

In this vacuum, too, one finds the motivation for the alarming but only too understandable suspicion with which 'culture' is regarded in ever-widening circles of our tumultuous world. It derives, undoubtedly, from that history of the Golden Ages of humanity I have briefly referred to: if, in the time of Pericles or the Medici, of Elizabeth I or the great Moorish rulers of Cordoba and Granada and Cadiz, culture was the prerogative of the aristocracy, to be emulated, later, in the wake of the French Revolution, by the bourgeoisie, how can it be regarded—at least by the Third World—other than with suspicion, doubt, or open rejection?

In a world threatened, on an ever more stupefying scale, with famine and disease, violence and war, refugees, tyrannies and oppressed multitudes, 'culture' may indeed threaten to become a dirty word, an obscenity. But only if we persist in continuing to think of culture as the reserve of royalty, of the idle few: NOT if culture is seen as the indispensable generator of meaning within society as a whole. In other words, only if culture is seen as a court dialect rather than a complex of languages adequate, and indispensable, for the expression of the totality of human experience.

If it is true that culture has, over many centuries, become identified with 'those who can afford it', then indeed it has little to offer to those struggling for existence on a physical level. What reply is a musical masterpiece to the hunger pangs of a child? What 'immortal' work of literature can break the chains of a slave? What comfort is a Rembrandt self-portrait to an oppressed woman?

But, of course, these are unfair equations. In fact, they are no equations at all. Hunger exists, and can only be overcome if the hungry are nourished by bread, not music. Bondage exists, and can be eradicated only by breaking all the innumerable chains, material and spiritual, which shackle the unfree. The acknowledgement of the full humanity of woman is not dependent upon painting. But not for a moment does this imply that humanity as such—as a whole, or within the context of societies, or as a host of individuals—does not *need* music, or literature, or painting (not to speak of education, of recreation, of science, of mental, emotional or spiritual stimulation). To acknowledge the need for culture is not to underrate the basic needs of human beings to survive, to be free, to improve their lot: it is only to acknowledge that humanity also requires meaning, or at least to set out in search of meaning. This need does not *replace* the need to be fed, to be free, to be able to work . . . but it establishes itself *alongside* those needs which peculiarly identify humanity as a form of life on earth.

If there is, and there is, resistance and animosity in the minds of many to the culture of the few, it probably results from efforts 'to bring culture to the masses': a symptom of the same missionary spirit that contributed to the decay of both Christianity and Marxism (both utopian in their teleology;

227

yet both excluding a vital part—either the material, or the spiritual—of the needs of the human person).

IV

It might be more appropriate to suggest that one should start from the other end and 'take the masses to culture'. But, in the light of my initial proposition, this misses the point too. 'The masses' (deliberately to use an objectionable term) do not find themselves 'over here'—and culture 'over there'. Culture is NOT a Golden City to be aspired to; a condition for which only the initiated may qualify. If it is to be approached as the centre of man's faculty (and the expression of his need) to produce meaning, it is as inherent to the human situation as language itself. It then becomes a matter of identifying its processes and possibilities, in order to establish those circumstances within which, as it were, meaning can emerge most meaningfully.

Violence is often seen as the antithesis and denial of culture, the Antichrist to the cultural Christ. Yet it seems to me both dangerous and a fallacy to divorce violence from culture. Especially in a world of tumbled ruins, which I have briefly tried to evoke, violence itself implies the production of meaning: it is society's way of saying, 'No!' It is meaning at its most emphatic—but, of course, also at its most destructive. *Violence is the language culture speaks when no other valid articulation is left open to it.* Once we have defined the true nature of violence (generally speaking, and within each specific context), a beginning might be made in turning this destructive expression of meaning into a positive current. If violence is the only utterance possible in a given human context; if murder and pillage are the only languages conceivable in a given situation, the problem lies not with violence but with the suspension of other possibilities of human articulation. Understanding violence may well be the first step towards an understanding of culture.

It is not a territory one can venture into with preconceptions or prejudgements. The pressure of violence may, in itself, stimulate counterforms of meaning. In South Africa, in the course of the last decade, there has been an explosion of poetic creativity amid all sections of the population—though the reasons for the sudden eruption of poetry may be vastly different in black and white communities (and, in the latter, in Afrikaner and English communities). For many Afrikaans writers poetry has become, in the face of censorship, a safe retreat from the much more exposed territory of fiction; English speakers, having lost their political power and much of their economic power after a century and a half of uncontested domination, find in poetry a—relatively harmless—domain within which the old muscles may now be flexed in a literary manner, in order at least to maintain an illusion of power. For black writers poetry is exactly the opposite: an instrument of liberation, a new language which exhilaratingly gives shape and meaning to Black Consciousness and an experience of unity that transcends all vernacular divisions: it is a means not of finding sanctuary from, or a surrogate for, political power, but of *confronting* it and of expressing it. This is culture at its most affirmative, and by no means limited to an exclusive élite.

In fact, what has been happening in South Africa in recent years, also serves to confirm the paradoxical and vital nature of culture: works written by black and white (English and Afrikaans) authors used to run in three more or less separate streams through South African history, a separation aggravated in recent decades by apartheid. But most recently, although each has maintained its unmistakable identity, all three currents have converged in a singular expression of joint resistance to oppression. What individual writers express is obviously determined primarily by private experience, temperament, hope and the frustration of hope: yet essentially all are involved in the same activity—not just of *opposing* a political regime, but of *affirming* lasting human values, and providing the open ends through which these can expand and continue to grow.

All are involved in the articulation of cultural languages, different in syntax, identical in essence. And what they have in common is above all the production of a particular kind of meaning derived from a search encountered in many other contemporary societies which have also experienced the collapse of old certainties. This is the search for roots, for the abiding human values which have become only temporarily obscured by personal political experience, or by the disintegration of the Great Systems. Perhaps these are values all culture inevitably returns to when it seems threatened by extinction, and from which nourishment must be drawn in order to continue into the future. It is a set of root-values which can be summarized by that meaning which is uttered in the birth of language: *I am: we are.*

Censorship and Literature

(1982)

I

The territory on which the private and the social meet has always been a highly charged magnetic field, and even more so when the private is represented by a creative individual. It cannot be otherwise. The individual needs the safety and security of the organized group; the artist finds in his community the sustenance, the reassurance of a tradition within which to express himself, and the public to which he must inevitably address himself if there is to be any meaning in his work. Society, on the other hand, needs the inspiration, the enterprise, the stimulation, the vision of the creative individual to open up new perspectives and possibilities for the future, a new insight into the present, and a valid interpretation of the past.

More than in any other art form, this relationship assumes particular significance in literature, because the medium in which the writer expresses his intensely individual view of the world happens to be the very medium in which society communicates. In this respect language is unique as a medium of artistic expression, differing radically from, say, the marble of the sculptor, the paint used by the painter, or the sounds employed by the composer. Language is a meeting place, a point of confrontation, between the individual and the social.

In primitive society these two worlds generally seem to operate in harmony; they may, in fact, be operating in such close association as to be practically inseparable. The primitive artist (who is, more often than not, also the scientist, the religious leader and even the legislator of his tribe) does not attempt to impose an individual view of the world on his people: on the contrary, he tries to act on behalf of his people as a whole; far from challenging the beliefs of his tribe he acts as their curator and guardian. His mind and work are the archives, the museum, the temple, the art gallery of his people. He does not act against taboo, but with it.

Problems arise as this primitive and homogeneous tribe begins to grow more complex—on the purely physical level, as a result of numerical growth and territorial expansion, as well as of occupational diversification; and on the mental and spiritual level as a result of the accumulation of new experiences, and the divergence of public functions (with the artist, the scientist, the theologian, the philosopher, the law-giver, the judge each developing in his own right, jealously safeguarding his own area of jurisdiction). Sooner or later a stage is reached where the private and the collective are no longer automatically in harmony; where tribal taboo may, in fact, threaten the enquiry of the individual mind.

Even in highly developed societies the relationship can be potentially stimulating and, in fact, indispensable for creative development. In the ideal situation the two great organs of society, Church and State, aiming at the commonwealth, maintain order and stability by ensuring the maximum amount of personal fulfilment for the maximum number of people; they honour the past by safeguarding tradition; they guarantee security by upholding the accepted and acceptable values of the group. In this way, society is essentially conservative; its watchword is the status quo. In this same ideal situation the writer (and the artist generally) prevents stagnation by defining new options; he is the agent of change, of exploration, of risk.

Neither can really do without the other. The artist on his own would introduce anarchy; the agents of society, if left unchecked, would become totalitarian. Or, defined in different terms, the artist, inspired by the ideal of freedom, would bring about a different kind of tyranny since each individual's total freedom would threaten everybody else's: whereas the ideal of justice that inspires society at its best would turn into its very opposite if it became an absolute notion overriding all the private interests of individuals.

Through an intricate system of checks and balances the artist and his society can, in the ideal situation outlined above, find a dynamic form of co-existence ensuring both personal and public growth. Unfortunately, of course, this ideal situation obtains very rarely, if ever. In the few most glorious moments of the history of civilization the wishes of the individual (as expressed by the writer) did seem miraculously to coincide with the aspirations of the nation and the interests of the group. In the great epics of Homer and Virgil this harmony is expressed admirably. But a time arrives when the individual becomes threatened to such an extent and on so many levels, that the artist has no choice but to turn against the organization and the interests of the organs of society: this situation tends to arise especially when these organs, transcending their function as means to an end, become ends in themselves. By the same token, in such a situation the organs of society, notably Church and State, feel themselves threatened by every dissenting voice and resort to repressive action in order to safeguard not society as such, but their own power-interests. This is when taboo, which fulfils a creative and possibly indispensable function in primitive society, expresses itself in the form of censorship: what used to be constructive and wholesome now becomes destructive and a symptom of sickness.

More often than not the change is slow and imperceptible:

for that very reason it is usually not perceived before it has gone so far that a violent confrontation is unavoidable. In South Africa the moment of change was announced quite dramatically in the historic clash between Verwoerd and Van Wyk Louw in 1966. Why, asked Verwoerd, should a writer feel driven to ask, *Wat is 'n volk?* ('What is a nation?')? What is required of the writer, said the Prime Minister, is not a question but an affirmation. While Verwoerd believed that we were still living in the epic age Van Wyk Louw realized that we had progressed beyond it. And it can be no accident that this clash more or less coincided with the introduction of official, codified censorship in South Africa.

II

It would be impossible fully to evaluate the impact of the threat of censorship to literature without attempting to define more clearly the function of the writer in society. Obviously aspects of this function may vary quite widely from one society to another, but it should not prove too difficult to clarify the essence of that function. In the light of the brief historical view offered above it would seem to me that the writer has retained something of the original function of the *shaman*. Certain aspects of this role have been taken over, in the process of diversification and specialization imposed by the development of civilization, by the scientist, the theologian, the philosopher, the teacher, etc. But, at the very least, the writer exercises his functions with a very special awareness of his allegiance to that essential dimension of human existence which can be defined as *meaning*.

The writer may in fact be regarded as one of the organs developed in the evolution of society to respond to its inherent (if often obscure) *need* for meaning—as vital to its spiritual survival as sunlight to a plant or water to a fish. It is the writer's responsibility to clear the access to these basics by constantly exploring the facts of his world and of his own experience and to correlate these subjective findings with what may be termed the 'fundamentals': truth, liberty, justice. Which means, quite emphatically, that the writer's function is not limited to aesthetics, but that it is, in the fullest sense of the word, existential, and rooted in morality.

Perhaps one should see the writer as a physiologist whose duty it is to explore as meticulously as possible the anatomy of an organism and probe the most hidden secrets of its processes and its needs, and to suggest the possibilities of meaning in the interrelationships of organs, parts and functions. His domain is that of meaning, not of healing. But unless he performs his function and performs it well, and unless his diagnosis is heeded, healing would not be possible.

His diagnosis makes known what has either been unknown, or only partly known, or even wilfully ignored in the past, and this defines the danger inherent in the writer's exploratory function. For society requires knowledge of itself, but it does not always consciously admit that need: its instinctive reaction may well be to be left in peace, rather than to be forced to acknowledge a state of affairs which will stir it out of the security of inertia into some form of action.

It is a hazardous undertaking, not only for the writer, but for the society that permits him to undertake his explorations. He may come up with uncomfortable facts which those in power might have preferred to remain hidden—either to prevent panic, or to strengthen their own position. In addition, the writer has no official mandate, no validity beyond his own allegiance to truth and liberty—and that can be easily manipulated by the unscrupulous to further their own ends. Even if our explorer is as honest as can be, his report remains a highly personal one, as it is based only on what he himself has witnessed. And he knows only too agonizingly well that his vision may be defective, that some error may have entered into his analysis, that the meaning extrapolated from his probing may be distorted in the formulation of his findings.

But this is the risk society must take if it allows the artist in its midst. It is either that—with, at least, the possibility of a more or less trustworthy diagnosis—or total ignorance about the body and its functions. A healthy society can face this risk; but if it is sick it may dread the vision of itself offered by an intrepid and impertinent individual. In this case a mortal sickness would remain undiagnosed.

III

In opposition to this function of the writer censorship represents all the repressive powers of society. If there is one fundamental aspect of censorship that has to be grasped before any of its effects on literature can be discussed, it is the fact that it never operates in isolation. Just as literature is not something apart from 'real life' but a vital ingredient of the total existence of the individual and of society, and in fact an area of interaction between the two, censorship is an integral part of a much larger and more complicated phenomenon. It represents the protective mechanisms and processes of the social organism in a state of excessive, cancerous development. Hence, in South Africa, censorship is only one part of an overall strategy which also expresses itself in such forms as detention without trial, arbitrary bannings, job reservations, the Group Areas Act, those clauses of the Immorality Act which prohibit miscegenation or any form of 'love across the colour bar', influx control, the frustration of black solidarity and stripping 9 million black South Africans of their citizenship through the creation of a mosaic of 'independent' homelands, the web of legislation controlling the press, and all the awesome secret activities of the Security Police. State Security, which in the healthy society is a means to an end, has become an absolute end in itself—and the vast fiction of a 'total onslaught' has been devised by the authorities to serve their own purpose, which is the totalitarian control of a heterogeneous, multi-racial, multi-cultural society by a small, power-drunk elite.

In the recent past (1981–2) the arrogance of power in South Africa has developed far beyond its own previous excesses. There had been forced removals of black communities before (involving some 3 million people), but seldom with the cynicism that characterized the demolition of squatter shacks around Cape Town in the midwinter of 1981; never with the disregard even for Parliament's own laws that marked the removal of Fingoes from the territory in the Tsitsikamma which had been ceded to their ancestors by the old Cape Government as a token of gratitude for their loyalty to white colonists during the nineteenth century. There had been incursions into Angola before, but never with the arrogance and futility of Operations Protea and Daisy late in 1981: and it is significant that most South Africans are deliberately kept in ignorance about the truth of these adventures. There had been deaths in detention before, but even after the shocking disclosures following that of Steve Biko in 1976 the circumstances surrounding the death of Dr Neil Aggett in February 1982 were particularly revealing of Security Police methods and arrogance. The abortive coup in the Seychelles, and the reaction of Cabinet Ministers in the wake of it, revealed a lot about a regime which in the past had made so much noise about the principle of non-interference. The 'revision' of security legislation, the official reaction to the De Lange Commission's recommendations on equal opportunities in education, and the advice of the Steyn Commission on controlling the media (blowing up the fiction of a 'total onslaught' to a giant balloon), shed some ironic light on the so-called 'reformist' policies of the Nationalist Government. The very first recommendations of that Government's own instrument of change, the President's Council, were disregarded, and District Six was not returned to the coloureds from whom it had been taken a decade before and which is one of the most brutal symbols of white arrogance in recent years.

Ever since Mr John Vorster, with such unseemly haste, exchanged the premiership for the State Presidency (treating that office, it seemed to many, as if a noble edifice were a common barn in which a rat might find refuge from the hounds of Information), there had been promises of 'change'; and the conditions for bold and creative fundamental reform were enhanced by the split in the National Party early in 1982, when Prime Minister Botha finally managed to rid himself of his extreme right wing— but instead of any really significant move towards change there has been a sickening show of pusillanimity on the Government's side, and an alarming hardening of attitudes on racial matters. The continuing war waged by the Security Police against newly legalized black trade unions, and the utter disregard for legality which accompanied the announcement of the intended cession of the black territories Ingwavuma and Kangwane to Swaziland (without any significant consultation with those concerned most immediately by the move), are indicative of the Government's contempt for legality, democratic procedures and ordinary human decency. One has the impression, in fact, that—despite the deceptively calm surface—the South African situation in 1982 is decidedly worse than during the Soweto riots of 1976. Indeed, attitudes have polarized alarmingly; and the amazing reservoir of goodwill and a willingness to co-operate, which for so long had characterized the attitudes of black leaders, even of radical ones like Biko, is now shrinking terribly, as, on the white side of the fence, fear and military 'preparedness' are escalating. A siege mentality has emerged quite chillingly from the relative openness of the 1970s, when one still had the impression that despite numerous sickening 'incidents' on the surface the basic *course* of society was moving in a positive direction.

(The situation is not yet *entirely* negative: from the increasing fermentation in Afrikaans academic circles, and notably the Dutch Reformed Church, which had previously provided the main moral justification for apartheid, something creative may yet emerge to temper the violence of the eventual transition towards majority rule, which is the historical imperative: but is there enough *time*, measured against the urgency of legitimate black aspirations and demands newly inspired by the liberation of Mozambique, Angola and Zimbabwe? Also, for the first time in its history, the National Party has accepted at least the *principle* of power-sharing: but are the cautious, fearful, half-hearted measures presently under discussion a sufficiently encouraging starting point—or simply a repetition of the Ian Smith syndrome of too-little-too-late?)

These are some of the circumstances determining South African society today: a society in which physical survival has become so important that it seems ready to sacrifice whatever spiritual and moral values might have informed it in the past. And these are the factors determining the operation of repressive machinery, of which censorship forms a part, or of which it is a symptom.

A specific and restricted exercise of censorship appears to me a natural function of educational or religious authorities. It would seem to me normal, even desirable, for a parent or teacher to 'grade' the reading matter of a growing child in order to meet the real needs of that child in his successive stages of emotional and intellectual development. I would even accept it as understandable for a church to warn its members against what it honestly regards, in terms of its own religious and moral ideology, as possibly pernicious writings. (Even then, I believe, a wise religious authority might feel that, rather than safeguard dogma within a rarefied and artificial climate, exposure to other ideas should stimulate healthy enquiry and strengthen belief.) But religious authority should not extend beyond this point: to overstep it

239

by actually banning works, or by prohibiting individuals from exercising their personal judgement would very soon become an intolerable infringement of personal liberty.

But when the State itself imposes censorship it becomes not a moral but a political act. And it comes as no surprise to note that censorship is invariably imposed by an authoritarian regime uncertain of its own chances of survival—either because it has just acceded to power, or because its power is threatened in some way. It was just as logical for Castro, or Mao, or Salazar, or Franco, or Verwoerd or the Ayatollah to impose stringent censorship (under the pretence of 'moral' considerations) as soon as possible after they had come to power as it was for the new 'open' regimes of Portugal and Spain in the mid-1970s to relax censorship. The fact that pornography is branded as 'communist infiltration' in South Africa and as 'Western propaganda' in some Eastern-Bloc countries suggests that morals as such have very little to do with the matter. The moment a political regime wants to impose uniformity of ideology and demands total submission, the need arises to control, above all, the thoughts of the people; and since political liberalization more often than not goes hand in hand with moral—notably sexual—liberalization, censorship becomes the accepted weapon of the authoritarian regime.

It may be regarded as forceful oppression of the individual's right to think and to decide for himself; an aggression against the free enterprise of the mind. In this sense censorship is part and parcel of the institutionalized violence employed by the State to keep itself in control.

IV

At first sight it may seem contradictory, in the context outlined above, to suggest, as many do, that censorship has been relaxed during the last few years, notably since the departure in 1979 of the previous chairman of the Publications Appeal Board, the unlamented ex-judge Snyman and his replacement by a young and more open-minded professor of law, Van Rooyen. (At roughly the same time a literary person, Professor A. J. Coetzee, was appointed Director of Publications.) Several facts appear to bear out the impression of relaxation. After banning Etienne Leroux's novel *Magersfontein, o Magersfontein* the Appeal Board, faced with the near-unanimous revolt of the Afrikaans literary establishment to whom Leroux had become an intellectual cult figure, reversed its previous decision. Nadine Gordimer's *Burger's Daughter*, banned in the second half of 1979, was unbanned three months later, followed by the lifting of the ban on my own *Dry White Season*. When we protested against the obscenity of exceptions being made of a few token white authors whose work happened to be widely known abroad, a ban on the anthology *Forced Landing*, by the black author Mothobi Mutloatse, was also lifted early in 1980. During 1981 and 1982 a number of major international literary works previously banned were also released, including that battle-scarred flagship *Lady Chatterley's Lover*. And in May 1982 my novel *Looking on Darkness*, banned on four previous occasions was also (conditionally) let through. Nudity in films is no longer automatically banned. At the same time, a number of significant shifts occurred in the criteria used by the censors to determine their decisions. Snyman's notorious 'ordinary man' was replaced by the more sensible concept of 'the likely reader'; a book is no longer banned on the basis of 'any part' being regarded as offensive, as in the past, but is evaluated as a whole; attempts have been made to 'grade' readership by prohibiting only readers under the age of eighteen to read particular books (a rule almost impossible to apply in practice, but which at least has the merit of shifting the onus of supervision from the State to parents). And whereas Snyman averred, in his judgement on Jack Cope's novel *The Dawn Comes Twice*, that 'the present

Act is concerned with the educational factor rather than the literary factor', and even went so far as to state that 'the very literary quality of the work can have the effect of bringing about the harm which the Act seeks to prevent' (*Burger's Daughter* and *A Dry White Season* were unbanned, *inter alia*, because they were found to be so badly written as not to fool or offend anyone!), the new dispensation allows for literary merit as some form of mitigating circumstance. (In practice, this approach could boomerang, however. In 1980 a committee of 'literary experts' led by Professor Merwe Scholtz ensured the reinforcement of the ban on *Looking on Darkness* by finding it wholly devoid of literary merit. The document, in crude English and with quaint reasoning, offers some priceless insights into the mental processes of whoever formulated it (not one of the panel members was English-speaking).

But does this imply that censorship in South Africa has undergone a definitive change? More important: would this imply that the movement towards political totalitarianism has been reversed or arrested?

There are a number of different factors to be considered. In the first place, whereas the application of the Publications Act of 1974 (as amended) has undoubtedly been eased in some carefully selected areas and cases, *the Act as such remains unchanged* and is still at the disposal of the Government whenever it should deem it necessary to invoke all its pernicious clauses.

Secondly, to put the recent trend of unbannings in perspective, one should look at what still remains banned. Among the literary corpses on the battlefield of some 20,000 titles prohibited in South Africa—*excluding* those of our entire generation of black writers silenced, with a single stroke of a bureaucratic pen, in the early 1960s and forced into exile—are names like Carlos Castaneda, Françoise Mallet-Joris, Emile Zola, John Updike, Robert Penn Warren, James Baldwin, Erskine Caldwell, Jack Kerouac,

242

Junichiro Tanizaki, William Styron, J. P. Donleavy, Vladimir Nabokov, Henry Miller, Alberto Moravia, Mary McCarthy, Brendan Behan, Nathaniel West, Guy de Maupassant, André Pieyre de Mandiargues, Colin Wilson, Jean-Paul Sartre, Alain Robbe-Grillet, William Burroughs, Jean Genet, Bernard Malamud, etc. etc. etc. Mutloatse's *Forced Landing* was unbanned: but Mutloatse was, at the time, a leading figure in the Soweto branch of PEN, with invaluable international connections: on the other hand, the moving and immensely important volume of short stories *Call Me Not a Man* by Mtutuzeli Matshoba—who does not have such international contacts—remains banned.

In the third place, if a certain cautious liberalization has indeed become evident, it arose from a confluence of very specific circumstances. The banning of *Magersfontein, o Magersfontein* alienated from the Government a significant part of its own cultural wing: by touching Leroux it had overstepped an invisible boundary, and the reaction among 'enlightened' supporters of the Party (including a number of persons prominent within the censorship machinery itself) was such that the authorities were taken by surprise. This coincided with an expression of unprecedented solidarity within the ranks of South African writers of all colours and languages, and a direct challenge to the Government that, unless something be done about censorship, we would simply emulate our colleagues in other countries of the world and go underground completely. The success achieved with the semi-clandestine distribution of *A Dry White Season*—getting 3,000 copies into circulation before the censors discovered its existence and banned it—proved both that we meant business, and that there was a good likelihood of succeeding with full-fledged *zamishdat*.

This occurred at a moment when the South African Government more than ever before was in desperate need of friends abroad. In England the Tories had just come to power; in the USA Reagan was becoming a distinct possibility; in Giscard d'Estaing South Africa already had a sympathetic ally. It would be most unwise, at that particular juncture in history, for the South African Government to alienate such desperately needed allies by cracking down forcefully on writers.

In addition, certainly in the past two years, the Government felt itself more immediately and urgently threatened by the development of black trade unions: compared with this the authorities may have felt, rightly or wrongly, that a threat from writers was of less direct and physical concern to them. This, too, may have played its role in what has been happening in censorship.

There is another consideration. In Italo Calvino's brilliant novel *If on a Winter's Night a Traveller* Director General Arkadian Porphyrich has this to say about the functioning of his police state: 'Let's be frank: every regime, even the most authoritarian, survives in a situation of unstable equilibrium, whereby it needs to justify constantly the existence of its repressive apparatus, therefore of something to repress . . . ' One should not underestimate the sophistication of the South African regime.

At the same time one should have no illusions about the Government's power to act. Censorship is only one cog in a vast machinery. There are more than enough repressive measures built into other Acts of Parliament for the authorities to *afford* a slight liberalization in the application of the Publications Act. Recent toughening of control of the media leaves one in no doubt about the real direction the Government has chosen.

As recently as June 1982, the Rev. Mzwandile Maqina of Port Elizabeth, founder of the cultural organization *Roots* and writer of such highly successful plays as *Give Us This Day*, *Trial* and, most recently, *Dry Those Tears*, was served with a banning order for three years (barely two months after the expiry of a five-year ban). In terms of this order, the playwright must be at home between 6pm and 6am, he must

244

report to the police once a week, he is forbidden to enter any educational institution or to attend any gathering (in South Africa, three people constitute a gathering); *and he is prohibited from writing anything for public consumption.* At the same time he may not be quoted in any manner. This means that his plays are also silenced. A Government which disposes of powers such as these, and which uses them in ways such as these, hardly needs a Publications Act.

Obviously it is much easier for the Government to silence a black man than a white. To cite only a few examples from personal acquaintance and from the recent past:

A young playwright writes and produces a play about the 'confusion' of a black man ensnared in the white man's laws: for some time, while the play is performed in the townships on a fly-by-night basis, it escapes the attention of the authorities, but then it is published. The book is banned outright, and soon afterwards the author is arrested, detained without charge for several months, and only released after his health has deteriorated so badly as to cause emphatic enquiries from writers and organizations outside. After his release he is 'banned', which means that he cannot retain his job. And his wife, too, is sacked by her employers because they do not want to be tainted by association.

Another young black man offers a few of his poems to the enterprising magazine *Staffrider* and is invited to join PEN. Immediately afterwards he is picked up by the Security Police, insulted, assaulted, and warned to steer clear of 'bad connections'. He relates his experience to other members of PEN and a few prominent writers lodge an official protest. This results in a swoop on the young poet's house: it is searched and left in a shambles; once again he is insulted and pushed around; and a final warning is issued: 'If you go back to your white friends to complain about this, you will disappear.'

A third black writer, a leading voice in the younger generation, who has already attracted a measure of public attention, is awarded an important scholarship to study in the USA—but he is refused a passport. Three applications in succession are turned down, in spite of formal protests by several writers' organizations, including PEN and the Afrikaans Writers' Guild. (In this case one can report a happy ending: the passport was issued at long last, evidently because pressure from abroad finally became embarrassing to the South African authorities.)

For obvious reasons the white writer can breathe more easily (although a special form of harassment is reserved for the Afrikaner dissident, because he is accused of stabbing 'his own people' in the back). But many outsiders seem to be unaware of the subtle forms of pressure which continue all the time—even in a climate of so-called 'relaxed censorship'. There is, after all, a special section of Security Police operations devoted exclusively to the monitoring of dissidents. It begins, for the writer, with the discovery that, simply because he is a writer, all his mail is opened and his phone tapped. And if it is relatively easy to adjust to it—and even to find in it a challenge to continue (since at the very least it suggests that one is taken seriously!)—it can become agonizing if the pressure extends to others. When a schoolteacher who innocently writes to me as a 'fan' suddenly finds herself confronted by the Security Police and threatened with the loss of her job simply because she has corresponded with me, it places a terrible burden not only on her conscience but on mine as well.

There is the strain of constant surveillance, even when one goes on an ordinary family outing; it is an eye-opening experience to return from a journey abroad and to be confronted, on the plane, by an individual who blandly gives one a catalogue of all the details of the trip and all the people one has met; and who concludes his chat with the wry announcement: 'Welcome back to South Africa'.

But of course one learns to live with that, as one learns to cope with the anonymous threats, by letter or telephone, against the members of one's family. If one is not prepared to live with it, one should either heed the censor or not write at all. There are other methods, too, all of them extensions of censorship: an 'invitation' to visit the Special Branch and 'discuss things'; and next time *they* are the visitors, arriving unannounced and with a great show of strength, to search one's house and confiscate notes and correspondence and even one's typewriters.

All of which places in particular relief the merits of the much-vaunted 'liberalization' of official censorship in the country. And it may be worthwhile to remind oneself of Etienne Leroux's recent warning: 'A puff-adder is never quite so dangerous as when it pretends to be dead.'

V

In one form or another, censorship persists. And it would be futile to argue that there is a case for 'reasonable censorship'; that one's fight is only against 'unreasonable censorship'. This is not casuistry: it is blatantly false. Censorship per se *is* unreasonable and pernicious. The nature of the threat it poses can be pinpointed in many ways, of which I summarize only a few.

1. Whereas the writer is committed to a process of discovering, probing, bringing to light, in order to evaluate experience and define its meaning, censorship operates from a premise of prohibition and closing down. In South Africa it forms part of a vast cover-up syndrome, of which the neurosis following the disclosures about the Department of Information scandals was only one symptom. The Government and its agents and agencies have embarked on an all-embracing strategy of keeping the populace in the dark about the truth of the situation in the country. The lie has become established as the norm: truth is the real obscenity. And this has percolated through to the level of the pub joke. More

247

than comic effect is involved when a certain Cabinet Minister is referred to as 'Mr Wolf'—because only Little Red Riding Hood can be expected to believe what he says.

2. While literature involves the whole territory of values and creativity both in private and communal experience, which implies that it is intrinsically non-violent (a pen, not a sword), censorship represents institutional violence at its most insidious.

3. Censorship, by its very nature, springs from a need to impose *mass values* and is aimed most especially against those highly individual questionings of mass values which are a hallmark of the work of creative writers. Censorship cannot make exceptions: the legislation from which it derives is inevitably based on a consideration of the 'generally accepted', the largest available common denominators—i.e. a denial of the creative mind which guarantees growth and development and mental health in a community.

4. To make it worse, these mass values are interpreted by a small group of appointed persons who have to act *on behalf of* others. In other words, in the administration of censorship there is, per definition, an absence of integrity in the most basic sense of the word: not the true convictions of the administrators are involved, only their vicarious experience, their—necessarily inadequate—interpretation of 'community needs' or 'community values' or 'community standards'. The motto of the censor is: 'I have no complaint against it personally, but think of all the others who may be harmed by it.' There is certainly no evidence that any of the multitude of elderly persons spending weeks, months or years on end viewing X-rated films or reading pornography has ever been depraved by it. But invariably 'the others' are used as a pretext.

Censorship rests on the premise that a handful of people have the right to decide what an entire society should read, see, discuss, and, in the final instance, think.

5. The moment official censorship is introduced, as

happened in South Africa in 1963, with a much more stringent Act passed in 1974, a large minefield surrounding its official operation is activated. The actions of the first Publications Control Board and its various successors (the numerous small committees, the Directorate, and the Board of Appeal) form only the nucleus of a cancerous cell which divides and subdivides and multiplies rapidly to endanger the whole body.

Because the definitions applied by the censor are, inevitably, extremely vague, no one can be sure in advance what will be banned and what not. The immediate result is that publishers grow exceedingly cautious (after all, they are the ones who run the greatest financial risk), and it may happen—as it has happened several times in South Africa— that manuscripts of particular merit or promise are turned down. Even when publishers may decide to risk publication, printers may be wary, or may be subjected to pressures of another kind. When Human & Rousseau decided to publish my novel *Lobola vir die lewe* (*Dowry for Life*) in 1962, while the original censorship Act was being debated in Parliament, at least one of the printers who turned it down did so because of pressure from a church which threatened withdrawal of its business from the printer in question.

Booksellers, too, become inhibited. And because there is no time limit in South African censorship (books have been banned after being in circulation for years) many dealers prefer not to buy any supplies—or only very limited supplies—of titles 'at risk'. At best, the long delays imposed on the supply of books from abroad, kept under embargo upon the whim of any customs official, add to the confusion in the trade.

Even writers themselves may become inhibited. For the last fifteen years or so I have received an average of two or three manuscripts per week from young aspiring writers in need of advice and comments: and by far the most alarming trend I have witnessed in recent years (notably since 1974) is that the first question a young writer puts in his accompanying letter is no longer: 'Do you think it's any good?' but 'Do you think it will get past the censors?'

Can it be coincidence that during the last decade only *one* new novelist of importance in Afrikaans (John Miles) and *one* in English (J. M. Coetzee) have made their appearance?

VI

One must be realistic. There is practically no society in the modern world where at least some form of censorship does not obtain. No human society presents an ideal co-existence of perfect people: restraints become inevitable from the very moment a group of individuals decide to live together. This was true even in such licentious ages as those of, say, Aristophanes, or Plautus and Terence, or Boccaccio, or Rabelais. In fact, some of these writers operated within the most awesome censorship systems the world has ever known. Nor should it surprise us, if we bear in mind the historical view offered earlier in the essay. To recapitulate briefly: society and creative individuals are indispensable to one another; each inevitably threatens the territorial integrity of the other—yet at the same time each offers a challenge and a stimulus necessary for the healthy growth of the other.

The operative word, it seems to me, is 'challenge'. And it may be a good idea to bring back into circulation the concept of 'challenge and response' in terms of which Toynbee interpreted the rise and fall of civilizations. Provided the social body is healthy, the explorations of the writer offer a challenge leading to constant reassessment of values and the possibility of growth. A sick body is too weak to respond effectively, its values being so tenuous that they cannot stand up to public scrutiny.

It is the opposite relationship that appears more significant in the present context: the challenge offered by society and its

250

instruments to the ingenuity, the will-power, the creative resources of the writer. When this challenge is reasonable it acts as an important stimulus to writers and other artists. Shakespeare did not only survive the threat of stringent censorship imposed by his society, but triumphed over it in such a way as to become the most glorious product of that very society. Chekhov succeeded in writing his masterpieces not only in spite of the challenge of czarist censorship but probably to some extent because of it: it was a threat which forced him to refine his sensibilities and to compose some of the subtlest plays in the history of the theatre. Solzhenitsyn represents yet another stage in the relationship between social or authoritarian challenge and artistic response: he was effectively barred from publishing, and eventually banished. The success of his response lies in the fact that the very measures taken against him have contributed towards turning him into a major writer in the rest of the world; moreover—and more important for the present discussion— Soviet censorship led to the widespread distribution of his work in Russia itself, in the form of *zamishdat*.

But a point may be reached when the forces of repression or oppression become so powerful that paralysis ensues: when, in other words, the challenge becomes so great that no response is possible. Even if this is only temporary, or effective only on the public level (i.e. by making it impossible for authors to publish), it means that an important form of mental nourishment for society as a whole dries up in the process, threatening the vitality of that entire society.

Ever since Plato it has been all too easy for authorities to underestimate, or even to ignore, the real function and contribution of the writer: to the censor the writer is either a nuisance or a luxury, not a vital organ of society. And if that mentality prevails the very life and growth of the community is threatened.

VII

In spite of the gloomy picture I have drawn, it seems to me that, in very specific and sometimes quite spectacular ways, censorship in South Africa has essentially *failed* when judged in terms of its own justifications.

1. Censorship tries to inhibit written opposition to the system. In South Africa this has, admittedly, succeeded up to a point. After the explosion of new talent in fiction in the 1960s the ensuing years saw a sadly diminished activity; and State-subsidized theatre, in spite of splendiferous new buildings and amenities, is almost moribund. But this is not the total picture. In black writing the past decade has seen an eruption of talent and vitality unrivalled in South African literary history. Much of it gets banned—but most of it is distributed in a wide variety of ways before a ban is imposed; and poetry readings and fly-by-night performances of plays reach an increasing audience. In fact, black writing has become one of the most important factors pushing for change (and directing that change) in South Africa.

Also, to compensate for the paucity of new voices among white writers, existing ones have acquired an increasing audience both in South Africa and abroad. My own experience may point to a larger trend: not only do my books sell more copies in South Africa than before they were hit by the censors (and bannings themselves obviously stimulate interest), but the threat of being censored in Afrikaans, which would effectively deprive me of my habitual readers, prompted me, as a measure of literary survival, to start writing in English as well. The result is that books previously available only in Afrikaans are now published in many different countries. And because they are in English they are now, for the first time, being read by black readers in South Africa too, as well as being translated into indigenous languages. In several countries—notably the USA, France and Sweden—a new awareness of South African writing has recently developed precisely because of the publicity given to the workings of censorship.

2. Censorship is aimed at isolating writers from one another through fear and intimidation. In South Africa the opposite has happened. For a very long time three different streams of literature ran their separate courses: black, Afrikaans and English. But during the last few years a new awareness of a common identity as writers has arisen, creating a new sense of solidarity in a body of informed and articulate resistance to oppression. The establishment of a Soweto-based PEN Centre was a culminating point in this development. (It is true that the Centre was closed down in 1981—in itself an ominous and depressing symptom of the deteriorating situation in the country—but one should not misjudge the event. Black writers turned away from PEN because of pressure from their society and their commitment to that society, not because as writers they themselves rejected co-operation with whites. In fact, in many ways and on many levels the association of writers of different races and cultures continues, and it is intensified by the awareness of a common enemy.)

It would be naïve to ascribe increased opposition to apartheid to censorship only, but in a complex situation censorship has become a significant catalyst in creating solidarity and in deepening awareness.

3. Censorship wants to alienate reader and writer from each other. Far from achieving this, censorship in South Africa has created for the reader a new sense of adventure in literature, a new sense of being 'in touch'. This is illustrated by the increased demand for banned books among white readers and in the way in which new publications by blacks are sold on the streets of Soweto. When the original Afrikaans version of *Looking on Darkness* was banned the public rallied by collecting thousands of rands (most of it contributed in sums of two or three rands by anonymous donors, 'ordinary readers') in order to fight the ban in the courts.

4. Censorship tries to reduce the writer to a state of impotence. But the establishment of a variety of writers' organizations (with the Afrikaans Writers' Guild, open to all languages and races, the most influential among them) testifies to the frustration of this aim. Writers have acquired a larger and more effective public forum since the introduction of censorship than ever before.

There is another telling example of the failure of censorship on this point: the fund referred to above, established to fight the ban on *Looking on Darkness*, was in fact used to launch the small private publishing enterprise Taurus which publishes any manuscript that runs the risk of being banned. A list of subscribers was established and when, in 1979, it became obvious that my novel *A Dry White Season* was in danger of being banned (in its Afrikaans version), 2,000 copies were quietly printed and despatched to these subscribers, followed by another edition within a week. By the time the censors pounced, as I mentioned earlier, there were enough copies in circulation to ensure a long clandestine existence.

The important thing was that a psychological victory had been gained and that, from now on, even young writers knew that their work could be published, whether in danger of being banned or not.

It is obvious that, with the formidable apparatus at its disposal, the government may close up existing loopholes in due course. But the writers now have the advantage of a head start and of having seen the power of the written word in action. At the same time censorship has failed to neutralize the writers, as a result of increasing international recognition of the work of some authors: which may not provide total 'protection' should the Government really decide to clamp down, but which certainly undermines both the efficacy of censorship and the credibility of the Government behind it.

5. Censorship is based on the concern to impose an ideology at the expense of the free circulation of ideas. And

South African society has indeed been sadly impoverished through lack of open contact with the ideas of the world outside. But at the same time censorship stimulates interest in what is banned. And the enthusiastic reception of work of dissident writers by the younger generation of readers (of all races) counters much of the ravages of censorship.

The writer does not primarily direct himself at 'changing the system' but at awakening the individual consciousness in such a way that eventually a change in the system becomes not only possible but inevitable. And the existence of censorship is aiding the process by lending greater resonance to the words of writers.

6. Censorship aims at maintaining the unity of the system. In South Africa the banning of certain works (notably Leroux's *Magersfontein*) has already placed some fervent disciples of the Government in an unbearable situation— loyal to the politics of the Government they yet find themselves constrained to defend both the aesthetics and the morality of a banned work. If one Government body bans a book and another awards it a prestigious literary prize, schizophrenia sets in and another crack appears on the granite face of the system.

7. A small yet significant afterthought: censorship is humourless. It cannot be otherwise. Yet few institutions in recent South African history have been so devastatingly ridiculed—not only by opponents but from within the *laager* itself—as censorship. The system has not been helped, either, by some of the personalities administering it during the Kruger and Snyman eras, or by some of the farcical contradictions in their decisions. In fact, every ban lifted in the process of liberalization, underlines the futility and farce (and the waste of taxpayers' money) involved in the original ban, and thereby undermines the system from within.

VIII

There is clearly no reason to rejoice: that puff-adder may only be *playing* dead. Two dangers lurk inherent in the new movement of liberalization itself: either it may create a false sense of security; or it may prompt the numbness of impotence, of being 'used' by the State for its own purposes, of being manipulated. And there is no doubt at all: those of us who are today allowed more freedom in publishing than before are *indeed* being used. But is that a reason to fall silent, and thereby play even more neatly into the hands of the powers-that-be? If there resides a core of truth in the work of a writer, that truth will reach out to others whatever efforts are made by the authorities to discredit, inhibit, restrict or distort it.

The only reliable gauge in the situation, as in all others, seems to me the conscience of the individual writer himself. He may not be able to prevent the authorities from trying to contain him by allowing him more scope. But the important thing is simply to *go on writing* according to the dictates of his conscience: to write what, through his own temperament and experience and the precarious light of his own insights, he believes he *must* write. The integrity of his work in itself provides the only available guarantee against manipulation from above—whether through restriction or through greater freedom of movement. If there does exist a larger breathing-space than before, it is imperative for that space to be exploited to its fullest extent—before the dark descends. The body is not only sick but ignorant of its ailment and its true needs: unless it be diagnosed in time it may well prove to be a sickness unto death.